Landscapes of the
PYRENEES

a countryside guide
Sixth edition

Paul Jenner and
Christine Smith

SUNFLOWER BOOKS

Sixth edition © 2011
Sunflower Books™
PO Box 36160
London SW7 3WS, UK
www.sunflowerbooks.co.uk

Evening near the Circo de Soaso (Walk 26)

ISBN 978-1-85691-397-3

Important note to the reader

We have tried to ensure that the descriptions and maps in this book are error-free at press date. The book will be updated, where necessary, whenever future printings permit. It will be very helpful for us to receive your comments (sent in care of the publishers, please) for the updating of future printings.

We also rely on walkers to take along a good supply of common sense — as well as this book — on their rambles. **Be aware that the category of difficulty for any walk, most especially in the central and western Pyrenees, can change dramatically according to weather conditions.** A walk in the central Pyrenees that is easy in high summer could be impossible in spring due to snow. A route in the western Pyrenees, easily found one day, may call for skilled compass work in heavy mist the next. If the route is not as we outline it, and your way ahead is not secure, return to the point of departure. ***Never attempt to complete a tour or walk under hazardous conditions!*** Please read carefully the notes on pages 38 to 44, as well as the introductory comments at the beginning of each tour and walk (regarding road conditions, equipment, grade, distances and time, etc). Explore *safely*, while at the same time respecting the beauty of the countryside.

Cover: Cascada de Cola de Caballo (Walk 26)
Title page: Sant-Miquel d'Engolasters and the mountains of Andorra (Walk 11)

Photographs pages 29, 111, 114-115, 116-117, 125, 132-133: Neil Hardy;
  pages 1, 8-9, 10-11, 13, 14, 15, 17 (bottom), 18-19, 20, 22, 24, 47, 49,
  51, 56-57 (bottom), 65, 70, 74, 75, 81 (bottom): John Underwood;
  cover: Dreamstime; all other photographs by the authors
Maps by Sunflower Books
Drawings by John Theasby
A CIP catalogue record for this book is available from the British Library.
Printed and bound in China: WKT Company Ltd

10 9 8 7 6 5 4 3 2 1

☀ Contents

4 Landscapes of the Pyrenees

Plateau de Sault

Preface

Words on a page work a strange magic. Words like Albères, Sault, Cadí, Ordesa, Brèche, Ossoue, Vignemale, Iparla, and Aspe may be meaningless to you today but, once you have experienced the tours and walks in this book, they will ever after disturb your sleep. Perhaps your days, too.

The Albères ... the hot sun of the Mediterranean, shady forests of cork oak, dolmens and vineyards. Plateau de Sault ... where birds of prey fill the sky, and the agricultural life of the Middle Ages can still be tasted. Cadí ... so remotely beautiful that life in a town may never be palatable again. Ordesa ... sheer canyon walls and on them the shadow of the lammergeier, Europe's largest vulture. Brèche ... the freedom of a high mountain frontier crossing without customs. Ossoue ... where marmots fight to the death. Vignemale ... the last great glacier of the Pyrenees. Iparla ... the adrenalin rush of a spectacular ridge walk.

Some other words have the power to make you sad. Aspe ... the valley of the brown bears, hunted to the very brink of extinction. Ibex ... once plentiful in the Ordesa, now extinct there due to hunting. Throughout this book we try to emphasise the environment in which you will be driving, walking and picnicking, because if that is not enjoyed by you and many others, there will be no force for its preservation. If you feel, as we do, that the wilderness of the Pyrenees is important, we hope you will add your voice to those who argue for conservation — for the lammergeier, the izard, the brown bear and, above all, for the habitat itself, without which no schemes for the conservation of individual species can have any chance of success.

Landscapes of the Pyrenees is principally a guide to the outdoors, but we have not neglected the work of man. In particular, the prehistoric remains, which include some of the most important painted caves in the world and a large number of dolmens, seem to us to be very much a part of the natural world that early man inhabited.

The book is divided into three main sections, each with its own introduction.

For **motorists** there are twelve car tours, all designed to give you a taste of the huge geographical diversity that, in the Pyrenees, can exist within a very small area.

For **walkers** there are sixty long and short walks described

5

in detail — some classics, some devised by ourselves — all chosen for their combination of superb scenery, wildlife, and historical and human interest.

For **picnickers** we have chosen a number of sites, both organised and 'wild' (for those who like a generous helping of *al fresco* with their cheese sarnies). All sites operate a *take-away* service — that is, you take away all your debris!

Enjoy the Pyrenees!

Pyrenees — the people

With its mountain domain stretching virtually coast-to-coast, there is a wide diversity of Pyrenean stock. In the west are the Basques with their immaculately white-washed homes, pink *frontons* and a rebellious reputation. In the east are the Catalans — passionate about 'home' and, to some degree, successful in their pursuit of independence. Here you will be faced with three languages to fathom — French, Castillian and Catalan. But a common factor of all these mountain people is a changing lifestyle. Although there are a few souls still forging an agricultural living from the high pastures, there is a new generation of mountain entrepreneur — shepherding tourists and husbanding giant hydroelectric projects in the shadow of the peaks.

Acknowledgements

We are indebted to the following for help in researching this book:

Marti Pujol i Gou of the Ajuntament in Vilabertran for his tireless pursuit of prehistoric remains in Spain's Alt Empordà;

Jean-Marc Abadie for lifting our sights above road level to discover the extraordinary life on the enchanted mountain of Pibeste;

Toby Oliver of Brittany Ferries for advice on walks in countryside directly accessed from the company's Plymouth-Santander service;

Jean-Louis Trescazes and the village of Gavarnie;

Neil and Rossella Hardy, proprietors of the outdoor equipment shop Telemark Pyrenees in Ax-les-Thermes, for updating the west coast walks and researching Walks 15 and 23.

Books

It should be emphasised that *Landscapes of the Pyrenees* is a guide to country-side exploration and should be used in conjunction with a standard guide such as the *Rough Guide to the Pyrenees*. More walks and tours in and around the Pyrenees can be found in other Sunflower 'Landscapes' guides: *Basque Regions of Spain and France* (eight tours and 32 walks); *Costa Brava* (six tours and 23 walks, along the coast and inland); *Western Provence* (11 tours and 36 walks, from the Pyrénées-Orientales to the Rhone). Also of interest is *Wild Spain* (Sierra Club), especially for its coverage of surviving wildlife and wilderness.

Marmot

Getting about

This is a countryside guide to *all* of the Pyrenees — to the wild and haunting scenery in France, Spain and Andorra, stretching some 400km between the Mediterranean and the Atlantic. Some of the tours and walks are entirely within one country, but many take you across borders — so a passport in your pocket is a must.

Unless you have a great deal of time, such scale demands a **car**. If you fly in, hire is easy throughout the Pyrenees, with rates generally a little cheaper in Spain — especially if you can make the most of a package deal. Petrol is also cheaper in Spain and Andorra. (Don't forget your driving licence, valid insurance, vehicle registration document, two warning triangles, spare bulbs, fire extinguisher, first aid kit and, if you don't have a Euro-style number plate, a GB sticker. For Spain you'll also need a reflective safety jacket, available from the AA shop at Dover or any garage in Spain.)

There are several useful **train** services, particularly those along the Mediterranean and Atlantic coastal strips and in the northern foothills. These include the Perpignan/Cerdagne line with its Petit Train Jaune segment from Villefranche to La Tour de Carol, and the Paris/Toulouse/Barcelona service which also stops at La Tour de Carol, giving access to Andorra and to the rack railway into the mountains at Núria.

Buses vary in their usefulness to the walker, since the timetables are often designed for locals coming down into the towns in the mornings and returning in the evenings. We suggest a number of the more regular services.

Coach tours can be a way of seeing the countryside and sometimes getting to walks, particularly for popular beauty spots such as Gavarnie and the Pont d'Espagne — or for shopping expeditions to Andorra.

Taxis, and their more rugged mountain counterparts, the **jeep-taxis**, will have to be used on some occasions by those who have no car, for example in the Parc Nacional d'Aigües Tortes and to get to the Barrage d'Ossoue for Walk 21.

At the beginning of every walk we give details of the public transport services available and provide a telephone number or web address for up-to-date information. If you cannot speak the language, contact the local tourist office or ask your hotel to make enquiries. Unfortunately, lack of space prevents the inclusion of timetables in this book.

☀ Picnicking

Official picnic sites are few and far between in the Pyrenees and often, where they do exist, they are *too* accessible (just beside a main road for example) and may be sadly littered, when compared with 'wilder' sites. We have deliberately restricted suggested picnic spots on the grounds that virtually the entire Pyrenean range is one wonderful picnic setting. However we have included a specific suggestion or two at the top of each car tour, for those who enjoy a little company in their *al fresco* dining rooms; see the '*P*' symbols on the maps.

Please try to take your own litter away with you — even where there are bins provided, these inevitably attract more donations than they can contain, with unpleasant results. And tidying up your deposit in a plastic bag is not the answer. We are always aware of crossing a mountain frontier even without the benefit of customs — in France they sling their bright blue plastic refuse bags, but in Spain the rubbish is less 'tidy'.

Fires: Never light a fire other than in one of the fireplaces provided at organised picnic sites. The Pyrenees have suffered some devasting bush fires over the years.

Eats: If cooking is going to be difficult — don't. Feast instead on the wide variety of continental cheeses, meats and of course breads which are readily available in the mountains. Buy your bread in good time — bearing in mind that in France many *boulangeries* close at 13.00 sharp, and in Spain many will remain closed for most of the afternoon. Even the largest supermarkets usually have a lengthy lunch-break, which can prove disastrous for the ravenous traveller.

Water: Drinking fountains *(fonts)* should be fine. Many mountain streams are not only safe, they are delicious — if you use common sense: never drink still or sluggish water; avoid any rivers where there is luxuriant water-weed growth or obvious pollution. Check your map to see if there is habitation above your stream, even a refuge or *cabane*. Avoid the water if there are plentiful signs of animals.

Once again we advise common sense in your dress — that is, sturdy shoes for walking, cover-ups, sunhat and, particularly in high mountain areas, sunglasses (the glare can be fierce).

All picnickers should read the country code on page 37 and go quietly in the countryside.

Car tour 3: At Maçaners you have this astounding view to Pedraforca — the forked rock — landmark of the Cadí.

☀ Touring

In the Pyrenees remote scenery can be enjoyed without even getting out of your car, especially if you are willing to drive on tracks. The Añisclo Canyon, the Yaga, the Cadí, Canigou — these and many more are places where a feeling of wilderness is preserved, despite access by road. Unfortunately that remoteness is under threat, especially on the Spanish side of the range, where EU money is helping to fund major road development.

Progress along the foothills of the Pyrenees is admittedly slow. You can drive coast-to-coast via the French motorway system in an afternoon, but to travel closer to the peaks means a traverse of three days *minimum*.

Because of the relative remoteness of many areas, there may be no snow clearance in winter on some passes. It may be June before some minor roads are open to traffic, and these may be closed again from November onwards, due to winter storms. If you are touring in early or late season, be sure to carry snow chains (available at low cost in supermarkets in France and Spain), or be prepared to modify your plans according to conditions.

The 12 tours in this book give a comprehensive picture of the entire range. The touring notes are brief: they include little

history or information readily available in other publications. *We concentrate instead on route-planning:* each tour is designed to give you an introduction to scenery in a particular part of the Pyrenees and to provide as much variety as possible. We want to show you our favourite landscapes in the Pyrenees *and take you to the starting point of some delightful **walks.***

If you are touring, consider spending the night en route, rather than trying to rush back to base. Several tours cross frontiers — so remember to take your passport! We recommend carrying it with you at all times, in case an unplanned border-crossing presents itself.

The large touring map is designed to be held out opposite the touring notes and contains, in a handy compact form, all the information you need to follow our suggested tours. Should you decide to purchase a larger-scale touring map, we can recommend 'Pyrénées' (Rando Editions/IGN; scale 1:400,000) or 'Pyrenäen mit Andorra' (Reise; scale 1:250,000). Due to the small scale of our map, we have included only those tracks that we have driven ourselves and found to be suitable for the majority of cars. Moreover, we suggest alternative tarmac roads for the owners of exceptionally large vehicles (or Porsches!). Average speed on tracks will not exceed 30kph/18mph.

Lack of space prevents us from printing the great number of town plans that would be necessary, so we give you clear guidance through all built-up areas in the touring notes. However, if you will be spending any length of time in the

Pyrenees, it's a good idea to have up-to-date Michelin hotel guides for France and Spain — if only for the wealth of town plans they contain!

The symbols used in the touring notes correspond to those on the pull-out map; see map key.

All motorists should read the country code on page 37 and go quietly in the countryside.

A typical village of the eastern Pyrenees — Eus, near Prades and the access road to Canigou for Walk 7

Car tour 1: THE ALBERES

La Jonquera • Vilajuïga • Roses • Port de la Selva • Llançà • Portbou • Cerbère • Banyuls-sur-Mer • Port-Vendres • Collioure • Argelès • Le Boulou

134km/83mi; about 5 hours' driving, starting on the motorway at Junction 2 (La Jonquera) and finishing on the motorway at Le Boulou. **Note: passports required**

Walks en route or nearby: 1-3

A tour accessible from anywhere on the Costa Brava, by joining the coastal toll-motorway A7/E15 and taking Exit 2 (La Jonquera) on the Spanish side of the frontier. The circuit combines the archaeologically and historically rich plains of the Alt Empordà with a long, twisty and consistently-attractive coastal drive, also providing the opportunity to compare Spanish and French wines, direct from the producers.

Picnic suggestions: Some 7km beyond **Vilajuïga**, on the road to Sant Pere de Rodes you will see, on the right, **Mas Ventós** (⊼) — a picnic area with ample parking. Tables and benches are shaded by pine trees with outstanding views southwards across the Bay of Roses. An excellent spot to meet up with friends doing Walk 1; see map pages 46-47. Further on along the intinerary, once on the coast, choose any beach that grabs your fancy. Your choice includes: **Llançà, Portbou, Cerbère, Banyuls-sur-Mer, Port-Vendres, Collioure** or **Argelès**. Sheltered coves or wide stretches of sand, plenty of nearby refreshment and WC facilities.

I f you don't object to a long day, this tour gives you the chance to make some interesting detours and perhaps take a swim at one of the popular resorts along the Côte Vermeille.

Take EXIT 2 (LA JONQUERA) off the A7-E15 motorway, turning right (south) onto the N11, following signs for FIGUERES. After 7km/4.5mi turn left onto the GI602 (signposted 'CAPMANY, ESPOLLA'). You are now on the 'wine and olive oil route' where every village has its *co-operativa*. Stop and taste at **Capmany, Sant Climent, Espolla, Rabós** or **Garriguella** (23km/14.5mi). From Sant Climent an excursion is possible to the castle of Requesens, while from Garriguella you could make a short detour to the castle/casino of Perelada (■). Just beyond Garriguella you can, if you wish, shorten the tour by turning left on the N260, direct to Llançà. We continue straight ahead, to **Vilajuïga**, where Walk 1 begins. *(From here you have the option of visiting Sant Pere de Rodes and the Mas Ventós picnic area — a*

detour of 14km return; see map pages 46-47.)
The main tour continues straight ahead on the GI604 for **Roses** (36km/22mi ▲ △ ✕ ♥WC), the largest resort on this stretch of the Costa Brava, at the north end of an immense curve of sand.
From Roses take the GI614 towards PORT DE LA SELVA. The road climbs up and over the mountains. *(From the summit, 12km beyond Roses, you have the option of a another detour — to Cadaqués, a picturesque and very different resort, made famous by the Catalan surrealist painter Salvador Dalí. Allow 10km return.)*
From **Port de la Selva** (56km/ 35mi ▲ △ ✕ ♥WC) you will now follow the coastal corniche to France. *(Just outside the village, a turning on the left presents you with a second opportunity to detour to Sant Pere de Rodes and Mas Ventós.)*

The rose-coloured dome of the church is clearly visible as we climb above Collioure on Walk 3.

After 6km, **Llançà** (62km/38.5mi ▲△✕🅿WC) lies a little inland of its fishing port, an ancient defensive measure against pirates. Walk 1 ends here.

From here the road to France is increasingly spectacular. Newly opened tunnels make this a pleasurable journey even in busy peak season, with fresh vistas at regular intervals. We follow the coast to **Colera** (△) and then climb steeply past rocky bays, some with their architect-designed homes, others so rugged that not even the most enterprising developer has yet had his way. Enjoy wonderful views of open sea and sheltered coves back to the Cadaqués Peninsula and Cap de Créus and ahead to the frontier at Cerbère.

There is a steep, bird's-eye view descent (🕼) into **Portbou** (76km/47mi ▲▲✕🅿WC), the final beach resort on the Costa Brava and a major rail terminus, before the road climbs again past the last petrol station in Spain to the frontier (🅿; open 24 hours a day from 15 June until 30 September, and from 07.00 until midnight the rest of the year). Your road is now called the N114 and winds uphill and down for 4km to the attractive port of **Cerbère** (83km/52mi ▲▲✕🅿WC), the rail terminus on the French side of the border, its network of bridges and viaducts providing a perfect setting for cops-and-robbers film chases. Between Cerbère and Banyuls you come upon a marine reserve, the first in France and in the Mediterranean as a whole. Notice too, that the viniculture is far more intensive than on the Spanish side (photograph page 51). **Banyuls-sur-Mer★** (94km/58mi ▲▲△✕

🅿WC), birthplace of sculptor Aristide Maillol (photograph page 54), is a fashionable resort. Walk 3 ends here — as does the French traverse of the Pyrenees.

Continue along the coast to **Port-Vendres** (102km/63mi ▲▲✕🅿WC), a major fishing harbour, and **Collioure★** (105km/65mi ▲▲△✕🅿🕇▮MWC), where Walk 3 begins. The town was the favoured summer resort of the Fauves or 'wild beasts' — notably Matisse (visit Céret, Car tour 2, to see the art collection). The Château Royal (▮M), an ancient fort on the harbour, houses both indoor and outdoor art exhibitions. Here there are stony beaches, some sheltered by the high walls of the fort and the church on the other side of the harbour, where you can lunch while watching the artists and fishermen going about their work.

From Collioure the road climbs up the last headland, leaving the Côte Vermeille behind and dropping down to the huge flat sweep of the Côte Radieuse resorts, beginning with **Argelès-sur-Mer★** (112km/69mi ▲▲△✕🅿MWC). From here you can take the main D618 back to the motorway at Le Boulou, but we recommend the more picturesque D2 among the northern foothills and vineyards of the Pyrenees to **Sorède** (119km/74mi), and then **Laroque des Albères** (122km/76mi △), followed by the D11 to **Montesquieu** (126km/78mi) and on to **Le Boulou** (134km/83mi ▲▲✕🅿) and the motorway.

13

Car tour 2: INTO THE MOUNTAINS

Girona • Banyoles • Besalú • Olot • Ripoll • Sant Joan de les Abadesses • Camprodon • Prats-de-Molló • Amélie-les-Bains • Céret • Le Boulou

183km/115mi; about 6 hours' driving. **Note:** *passports required*
Walks en route or nearby: 4-9
An all-day circular tour, beginning and ending on the motorway, and therefore easily accessible to visitors from anywhere along the Côte Vermeille/Costa Brava, this excursion includes some of the most important

historical sites in the eastern Pyrenees and some very spectacular scenery — in both France and Spain.
Picnic suggestion: At **Banyoles** follow signs for 'Estany (Lake) de Banyoles' (⊼). Limited benches and tables available; the picnic area is signposted.

T he Pyrenees of history and pre-history provides the theme for this tour — Banyoles, with the remains of pre-Neanderthal Man, up to 200,000 years old; Besalú with its ancient Jewish quarter; Ripoll, founded by Wilfred 'the Shaggy'; and Sant Joan de les Abadesses, home of his daughter. Take time, too, to walk around the attractive walled town of Prats-de-Molló.

Leave the motorway at JUNCTION 6 FOR 'GIRONA NORTH' and then follow signs to **Banyoles**★ (18km/11mi 🏔🏖⚊△✕🚐M). Either skirt the pretty — though usually crowded — lake around the western shore (follow signs for 'ESTANY'; ⊼), or continue to Besalú directly by the main road along the eastern shore. (If you are already familiar with Besalú, a third option is to take the road to Mieres and Santa Pau instead. This is a slow but fascinating route through the heart of the Garrotxa (pronounced Garrocha), the volcanic region illustrated in the photographs on pages 56-57 (Walk 4). You would rejoin the main tour at Olot.) At **Besalú**★ (32km/20mi ☦🖼🏖✕🚐) stop to walk across the old bridge shown opposite and inside the walls of this living museum.
Just before **Castellfollit de la Roca**★ (☦✕🖼M) turn off for Montagut and Sadernes if you want to do Walk 5 or 6. Continuing on, you can bypass Castellfollit via the spectacular new

bridge and tunnels, but we recommend you go in to see the old houses perched dramatically on sheer basalt cliffs over the River Fluvià. At night, floodlights emphasise the fluted rock.
Olot★ (52km/32mi 🏔△✕🚐M) can also be bypassed, but the Museu Comarcal is worth seeing, for its collection of *Olot School* painters. Parking for Walk 4 is some 3.5km southeast of the town, on the GI524.

The Monasterio de Santa María at Ripoll

14

Canigou from the north; below right: the bridge at Besalú

The main tour continues from Olot towards VALLFOGONA on the N260, the alternative 'scenic' route to Ripoll, along a road which climbs dramatically through tree-drenched hills to the **Coll de Caubet** (1010m/3310ft 📷), where there are magnificent views north and south. Beyond **Vall-fogna** (🏚🍴), **Ripoll★** (85km/53mi ⛽🏚⛺🍴🅿WC) is an essential stop for its Monasterio de Santa María, founded in 879 by Wilfred the Shaggy.

Readers using the car tour as a stepping-stone to the west can now continue on the N152 to Ribes de Freser (and the setting for Walk 9); otherwise leave Ripoll on the C26 for **Sant Joan de les Abadesses★** (⛽🏚🍴🅿M WC), one of the most remarkable sights of the area and home of Wilfred's daughter, Emma, who founded an important monastery in the 9th century.

Continue to the small mountain town of **Camprodon★** (112km/70mi 🏚🏚⛺🍴🅿WC), birthplace of the Catalan composer Isaac Albéniz. From here climb steeply — we almost ran off the road when we spotted the rare short-toed eagle — to the **Col d'Ares** (1513m/4965ft 📷), bleak despite its relatively low height. The road then descends just as steeply to **Prats-de-Molló★** (144km/90mi

🏚🔺⛺🍴🅿WC) with its fortified walls and huge square, frequently the scene of *boules* tournaments.

You are now in the **Tech Valley**, a region also known as the Vallespir, with the magnificent Canigou massif to the north. Just before **Arles-sur-Tech** (164km/102mi 🏚🔺⛺) those wanting to ascend Canigou by Walk 7 or the Carança by Walk 8 should turn left to CORSAVY, VALMANYA and PRADES. The **Gorges de la Fou** are also on the outskirts of Arles — worth visiting, but see also Tour 4 for gorges you don't have to pay for! Continue along the Tech Valley by the D115 to the busy spa town of **Amélie-les-Bains★** (167km/104mi 🏚🔺⛺🍴🅿WC) and, 8km beyond it, turn right into **Céret★** (🏚🔺🍴🅿M) to see the collection of paintings by the Fauves (mentioned in Car tour 1). Then return to the D115 and rejoin the motorway near **Le Boulou** (183km/115mi).

15

Car tour 3: TO THE CADI

Andorra la Vella • La Seu d'Urgell • Bellver • Llívia • Túnel del Cadí • Guardiola • Saldes • Gósol • Tuixén • La Seu d'Urgell • Andorra la Vella

210km/130mi; about 5 hours' driving. **Note: passports required**
Walks en route or nearby: 8-11
One of the most beautiful car tours in this book, passing along the dramatic north face of the Serra del Cadí and then plunging into the very heart of the Cadí-Moixeró Parc Natural.
Picnic suggestions: There are two especially good organised picnic sites in the Cadí, near the setting for Walk 10. Just west of **Saldes** you will see signs for the *'REFUGI LLUIS ESTASEN'*. Drive up this track, to see another sign on your left: *'LA SERRA AREA RECREATIVA 2,5KM'*.

Bear left at the first fork and continue uphill to the picnic sites (☐; full facilities including barbecues and WC). The **Mirador de Gresolet**, with wonderful views over the Serra del Cadí, is not far beyond the picnic areas. From **Gósol** take the road towards TUIXÉN and after 2.3km/1.4mi follow a track to the right, signposted *'FONT TERRERS'* (☐). Continue for a further 0.7km/0.4mi. Here, on a shoulder, in a delightful setting with views of the Serra del Cadí, are tables, benches and a barbecue. See map page 71.

This tour is a favourite of ours on account of its old stone buildings, its magnificent mountains, riverside picnic spots, and fabulous colour scheme (you'll see what we mean!). You will visit some 'forgotten' villages, where time has stood still.

If you are staying in **Andorra la Vella★** (☗🏔🏔✕🅿WC; Walk 11) or nearby, take the CG1 south* to the border, where the road becomes the N145, and continue to La Seu d'Urgell (other readers join this circular route at the most convenient point). At the approach to **La Seu d'Urgell★** (21km/13mi ☗🏔🏔✕🅿M) turn left on the N260, following signs to *'BARCELONA/TUNEL DEL CADÍ'*. As you drive along the broad and luxuriant **Segré Valley**, the

*You may prefer to leave Andorra la Vella and head first towards France, via the **Port d'Envalira**. The road in this itinerary climbs through magnificent scenery to the highest road pass in the Pyrenees (but alas, traffic is heavy, with many commercial vehicles). Once over the border and onto the N20, head south for **Bourg-Madame** and **Puigcerda**, where you can pick up the main tour.

dramatic north faces of the Cadí summits are on your right — you will be returning through the Cadí later in the day. *(After 24km you come to a left turn to Lles (45km/28mi) (📷) a famous viewpoint which you could visit as an 18km return detour.)*
The main tour continues for another 3km to the attractive hilltop village of **Bellver de Cerdanya** (48km/30mi △✕). Continue towards PUIGCERDA and, 3km beyond Bellver, ignore the turning right for the Túnel del Cadí, keeping on the N260 (but if you wish to do a short-cut and miss Llívia, taking this right turn will save 35km/22mi). At the roundabout in front of the border post at **Puigcerda★** (66km/41mi ☗🏔🏔✕🅿WC) take the **Llívia★** (71km/44mi ☗🏔🏔✕🅿M) exit, soon entering this historic Spanish enclave in France. From here you could continue east to the N116, to reach Walk 8, but the main tour

Josa del Cadí

returns to Puigcerda (76km/47mi). Follow signs through **Alp** for the TUNEL DEL CADI. (Or, for Walk 9, turn left at Alp for RIBES DE FRESER.)

The **Túnel del Cadí** (94km/58mi; a charge is made) is over 5km long and takes you under the high peaks of the Cadí to emerge near **Greixer** (102km/63mi). Continue on the main C16 to **Guardiola** (108km/67mi ▲✕⛽). Some 1km beyond Guardiola turn right (signposted 'SALDES'. After crossing the Saldes River, the road winds up to a shelf along the southern edge of the **Parc Natural Cadí-Moixeró**. At **Maçaners** (Massanes) you have the wonderful view (📷) of **Pedraforca** shown on pages 8-9 — the twin-peaked mountain that is as much a symbol of the region as the park's official black woodpecker. Beyond **Saldes** (126km/78mi ▲△✕⛽⛩) the landscape is increasingly 'Wild West', with red-rock gulches (📷).

Walk 10 ascends Pedraforca from **Gósol** (136km/84mi ♜▲✕⛩; photographs pages 72-73). This little village inspired the young Picasso, and a plaque on a house in the Plaça Major (square) commemorates his stay. You are now in the heart of the park, with a good chance of spotting izards (especially if you follow Walk 10), red and roe deer, partridges and golden eagles.

Beyond Gósol the road climbs to the **Coll de Josa** (1625m/5330ft 📷), where there is a panoramic view of the Serra del Cadí and its highest peak, the Canal Baridana (2642m/8665ft). As you drop down to the Josa River and the engaging hilltop village of **Josa del Cadí** shown above, you are deep in the park. At **Tuixén** (150km/93mi ✝▲✕) turn left over the bridge to explore the village, otherwise follow signposts to 'LA SEU D'URGELL'.

The road now continues past a succession of old stone-built villages — **Cornellana**, **Fórnols**, and **Adraén**, just beyond which the road begins to descend northwards, opening up views towards Andorra ahead and along the spectacular north face of the Cadí behind. Finally the road drops down into the Segre Valley back at **La Seu** (189km/117mi), from where you can return to **Andorra la Vella** (210km/130mi).

View south to the Serra del Cadí from the N260 east of La Seu d'Urgell

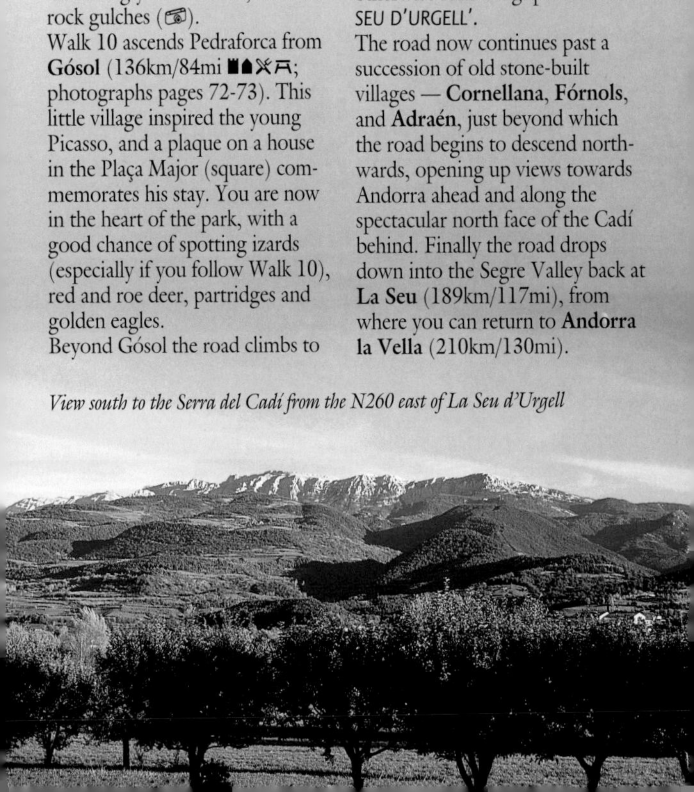

Car tour 4: THE PLATEAU OF THE CATHARS

Tarascon-sur-Ariège • Col de Marmare • (Montaillou) • Comus • Pas de l'Ours • Plateau de Sault • L'Espine • Montségur • Roquefixade • Foix • Tarascon-sur-Ariège

130km/80mi; about 4 hours' driving
Walks en route or nearby: 12-16
This circular tour, which begins and ends at Tarascon-sur-Ariège, visits one of the most remote regions in France, the last medieval stronghold of the Christian religious sect known as the Cathars — 'the pure ones'. It includes a section on good, but very narrow track, which is not recommended for nervous motorists. (To avoid this, after visiting the Pas de l'Ours, return to the D613 and head east, then take the D29 north to La
Bunague.) If approaching the region from the south, it may be more convenient to join the tour by taking the road out of Ax-les-Thermes that climbs up to the Col de Chioula via Ignaux. **Note:** *Between the main centres there is little in the way of petrol or refreshments.*
Picnic suggestions: From **Comus** the 'Route des Sapins' leads to the Col de la Gargante (3km), the **Pas de l'Ours** (3.6km) and an 'Aire de Picnic' (10km). See caption below and map page 80.

Birds — some of them quite rare — outnumber human residents in this remote area of the Pyrenees. Below ground, pot-holers are in their element. But apart from ornithologists and speleologists, this tour offers exciting vistas for the ordinary motorist, including an impressive canyon.

From **Tarascon-sur-Ariège** (🏨🛒🏠 ✕🚉; Walks 14-16) drive north on the D618 and, after the village of **Bompas** (3km/2mi), take a right turn onto the D20 (signposted 'ARNAVE' and 'COL DE MARMARE'). The narrow road climbs to magnificent views of the **Ariège Valley**, at **Axiat** passing below the talc quarry at Trimouns. Carry on to the **Col de Marmare** (1361m/4465ft; 36km/22mi), where the road joins the D613 coming up from Ax-les-Thermes. (If you are taking any walkers to Mérens-les-Vals, where this Walk 12 begins, turn right here: Mérens lies some 8km south of Ax-les-Thermes on the N20.)
You are now on the edge of a huge and wild plateau, one of the least known corners of France,

where vultures, buzzards and kestrels soar and dive for prey and sometimes simply play, happy to ignore the passing motorist … unless you stop. Then they are off.

The Pas de l'Ours, with its wonderfully vertiginous view over the Gorges de la Frau (Walk 13), is a splendid picnic spot. But there is nowhere to park. Park at the Col de la Gargante and walk the 600m to this pass (map page 80).

You can see your narrow road snaking ahead for miles.

Just beyond **Prades** (40km/25mi 🏠📷✕🚐WC) reach the turning left for **Comus** (43km/27mi 📷), the starting point for Walk 13. *(Not far beyond the Comus junction, a turn-off on the right leads to Montaillou, once an important village for the Cathars. If you visit Montaillou, double back and return to Comus.)*

Continue through Comus on the D20, signposted *'ROUTE DES SAPINS'*. The road gives way to track, which is amply wide at first. Some 3km from Comus you reach a junction at the **Col de la Gargante**, where there is ample parking. Beyond this point the track becomes very narrow. If you are taking the alternative route (D613/D29), first park and walk to the Pas de l'Ours, to enjoy the view shown below.

Whether by car or on foot, at the col *ignore* the track turning sharp right; *ignore also* the track straight ahead signed 'Point de vue 0,7km'. Take, instead, the level track to the left signposted *'ROUTE DES SAPINS'*; in 600m it brings you to one of the most awesome views in Europe at the **Pas de l'Ours** (📷), where there is a 600m/1970ft sheer drop into the Gorges de la Frau (Walk 13).

From here the single-lane track follows a narrow well-wooded ledge, with unprotected edges, but driving is easy ... *unless you meet someone coming from the opposite direction*. After stopping to see the view, continue on the track, which descends past a small forest refuge and then swings away from the gorge. Some 6km beyond the Pas de l'Ours come to a sign denoting the end of the **'Forêt Domaniale de la Plaine et de Comus'**, where another track joins from the right (from Belcaire). Continue until you reach another divide: here ignore 'Aire de picnic 200 metres' signposted to the left (unless you want to stop at an organised picnic site; ⛱). Instead turn right into a remote valley, from where you can enjoy views of distant toy-size farmhouses. The next fork, met

Montségur (top) and autumn colouring on the Plateau de Sault (below)

At **Fougax-et-Barrineuf** (73km/45mi) turn left onto the D9 towards 'MONTSEGUR'. This is the most attractive route to this famous castle, and the dramatic outline of the stronghold atop a pinnacle mountain soon looms into view ahead. You can't help but wonder how men achieved the 'impossible' task of importing the materials and then building such a magnificent structure. Following the steep-walled road, you appreciate how effective the watchtower high above you must have been against the enemy. The road climbs to **Montségur** village (81.5km/51mi ✕MWC) and on up to the castle★ (■), where the Cathars were besieged for ten months in 1243/44 and eventually massacred.

Some 4km beyond Montségur, ignore the turning left to Mont d'Olmes (it's 14km along the D909 to this ski resort, if you wish to visit it) and continue ahead for 'FOIX 26KM'. At **Montferrier** (87.5km/55mi) turn right towards LAVELANET but, on approaching Villeneuve d'Olmes, take a left turn for FOIX. This brings you to the D117, where you again turn left. Then, within 1km, take the turning off right — onto the D9. Heading towards Foix on this higher, more picturesque route through steep fields and rickety barns, you drive below the castle of **Roquefixade** (96km/60mi ■). Continue on this upper road, ignoring all turn-offs to the left. At the junction with the main N20, turn right for **Foix★** (113km/70mi ■▲▲♦✕🅿🚐⊕MWC). After visiting Foix, where the famous castle towers above the ancient history-rich town, the circle is completed by following the N20 to **Tarascon-sur-Ariège** (130km/80mi).

after a further 5km/3mi, offers three choices: ignore branches to the right (to Trasoulas) and the left (poor surface); continue ahead, skirting the village of **La Bunague** on your left. Eventually you come to a T-junction with the D29 (60km/37mi) and turn left. You are now driving along the edge of the **Plateau de Sault**. After 3km/2mi on tarmac, turn left onto the first tarmac side road you come to after La Bunague ... very narrow and badly potholed — but tarmac nevertheless. After 1km or so, ignore a turning marked 'Chemin Privé'. At **L'Espine** (72km/45mi) you emerge from dense forest and turn right *(however, the diversion of 4.8km left into the Gorges de la Frau should be taken if you've missed Walk 13).*

Car tour 5: DEEP VALLEYS, HIGH PEAKS, PAINTED CAVES

Tarascon-sur-Ariège • Grotte de Niaux • Aulus-les-Bains • Seix • Vallée de Bethmale • St-Girons • St-Lizier • Massat • Bédeilhac • Tarascon-sur-Ariège

168km/104mi; about 5 hours' driving

Walks en route or nearby: 14-16

A circular tour through the deep valleys and over some of the bleak passes that characterise the Ariège; the route visits two of the most important prehistoric painted caves in the world. Note: Tour 5 can be linked with Tour 4 at Tarascon-sur-Ariège.

Picnic suggestions: From **Vicdessos** take the D8 signposted 'Auzat' and continue for 11.3km/ 7mi to the Etang de Soulcem. Here, in an idyllic setting, close to the **Soulcem River**, are tables and benches (⊞). Walk 14 sets out from here (see pages 82-83). Beyond the **Port de Lers**, the **Etang de Lers** is a small and pretty lake much loved by the local population for boating and picnicking in the summer. It's set in the heart of wild mountain country — *but note: there is no shade at the lake.*

Brown bear and lynx! On the high plateaux of the Ariège-Pyrénées, a few still survive the insensitivity of the 21st century. Here, where the range is at its most tortured, the ecology of the uplands (including two 3000m/10,000ft-high peaks, Montcalm and Estats) has been protected from the cave-people and the car-people alike by the plunging depth of the valleys.

At **Tarascon-sur-Ariège** (♙♙♙ ✕🚆; Walks 15 and 16) take the D8, signposted 'VICDESSOS'. You quickly pass through **Niaux** (5km/3mi ♙♙ ✕), from where you can visit the famous **Grotte de Niaux★** (∩) set in the grey water-striped cliffs of the region, the less well-known Grotte de la Vache (∩), and the Musée Paysan (**M**).

Just before Vicdessos, the left turn to 'Dolmen Sem' is a short but worthwhile diversion, with spectacular views. In **Vicdessos** (14km/9mi ♙♙ ✕) turn right on the D18 towards 'AULUS-LES-BAINS'. *(Or continue on the D8 for Walk 14 or a picnic at the Soulcem dam; allow 23km return.)*

The D18 climbs through wild country to the **Port de Lers** (1517m/4975ft; 26km/16mi 📷). In that desolation you see to the south, the bear and lynx cling to life above the abyss of extinction. Climb through holiday country of deep woods, walking trails and weekend cabins noticeably unadorned by television aerials, and drop down to the **Etang de Lers**, a much-loved boating and

Cave paintings, Grotte de Niaux

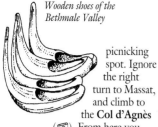

Wooden shoes of the Bethmale Valley

picnicking spot. Ignore the right turn to Massat, and climb to the **Col d'Agnès** (📞). From here you descend some 900m/ 2950ft, from high mountain country of bleak peaks and basin lakes to the depths of the **Garbet Valley** and to the narrow streets and tall buildings of **Aulus-les-Bains** (40km/25mi ▲▲✕). This cool old spa town is, unfortunately, infamous for the decimations of its hunters and bear-tamers.

From Aulus climb steeply out of the valley once more, following signposting to the **Col de la Trappe** (45km/28mi ▲▲✕). *(Just 1km from this pass you could make a 10km/6mi round-trip diversion left to Guzet-Neige; △📞 — highly recommended for the views you will enjoy back along your route, down to Aulus in the east and around the in-creasingly gentler mountains at the edge of the Pyrenees.)* The main tour continues along the narrow **Ustou Valley**, at the end of which you turn right, following signposts to 'SEIX'.

Seix (65km/40mi ▲▲△✕🛒) is a curious town astride the Salat River and a major centre for canoeing. (If you want to shorten the tour, in Seix follow signs straight on for St-Girons: cross the D32 and continue to the D618, there turning right for Tarascon — making a total round trip of 130km/81mi.)

Cross the river and take the D17 which drops down into the **Bethmale Valley** at the **Col de la Core** (1395m/4575ft; 📞). This was once a thriving agricultural community. Having been

abandoned and reverted to nature, it is now repopulated with holiday retreats. At **Castillón-en-Couserans** (93km/58mi ▲▲▲△✕🛒) turn right for **St-Girons** (106km/66mi ▲▲✕🛒WC), from where you take the main road towards SALIES for a visit to the Roman town of **St-Lizier★** (108km/67mi ✝▮), with its two cathedrals and surviving fortifications.

From St-Lizier return to St-Girons and then leave this busy town on the D618, signposted 'MASSAT' and 'COL DE PORT'. The road now takes you through the **Gorges de Ribaouto** and the **Gorges de Biert** to **Massat** (138km/86mi ▲▲✕🛒). Cross the Arac River and ascend through forest to the **Col de Port** (1250m/4100ft). Then descend to the vast cave★ of **Bédeilhac** (∩) with its paintings and engravings from the Magdalenian period (more than 10,000 years ago) and to **Tarascon-sur-Ariège** (168km/104mi).

The Noguera Pallaresa, the most powerful river in Spain (Car tour 6)

Car tour 6: PARC NACIONAL D'AIGUES TORTES

Vielha • Port de la Bonaigua • Espot • Parc Nacional d'Aigües Tortes • Gerri de la Sal • La Pobleta de Bellvei • Pont de Suert • (Caldes de Boí) • Túnel de Vielha • Vielha

215km/133mi; about 6.5 hours' driving

Walks en route or nearby: 17
A huge circuit along the Val d'Aran and into the Parc Nacional d'Aigües Tortes, one of two national parks in the Spanish Pyrenees.

Picnic suggestion: Continue through **Espot** (provisions) following signs for 'Parc Nacional d'Aigües Tortes' and 'Estany (Lake) de Sant Maurici'. Park at the **Prats des Pierrós** and picnic on the path to the lake or take a jeep-taxi to the **Estany de Sant Maurici** itself (ample shade). At the nearby Refugi Ernest Mallafré (15min on foot; see Walk 17 and map on page 89) it is possible to obtain refreshments and light meals.

Until the building of the Túnel de Vielha in 1948, the Val d'Aran was one of the most remote valleys in the Spanish Pyrenees, cut off from Spain every winter. The flowers and the rare butterflies (including the alpine grizzled skipper and the chequered skipper) are a testament to its former remoteness; the new electricity pylons a testament to insensitive development.

Leave **Vielha★** (✝🏔🏠🔺✕🍴M) by heading eastwards along the valley on the C1412, following signs for BAQUEIRA-BERET, and soon passing the right turn for Vielha's ski resort, La Tuca. If you have the time, many of the ancient villages in the valley are well worth visiting — Arties (parador 🏠), Salardú (✝🏔✕) and Tredos especially. From **Baqueira** (🏠✕) the road ascends steeply from the sadly disfigured valley floor below to the **Port de la Bonaigua** (2072m/6800ft; 22km/14mi 🚗), south of which lies the Parc Nacional d'Aigües Tortes. From the pass, the road (now C142) drops steeply to **Esterri d'Aneu** (46km/29mi 🏠✕🍴) at the head of the the **Noguera Pallaresa**, the most powerful river in the country. After 6km, just south of Guingueta, turn right and drive up to **Espot** (59km/37mi 🏠🏠🔺✕) and the entrance to the **Parc Nacional d'Aigües Tortes** (the **Prats des Pierrós**; 68km/42mi), from where a jeep-taxi can take you up to the

starting point for Walk 17. 'Aigües tortes' means, literally, 'twisted waters' — an irony now that hydro-electric schemes have straightened and controlled them. But away from the dams and pipes, izards still graze and golden eagles soar over the forests of fir, beech and birch shown on pages 88-89.

Return to the main road and continue south along the banks of the wide and powerful Noguera Pallaresa (where the photograph opposite was taken) to **Llavorsi** (96km/60mi 🏠🏠✕🍴) and **Gerri de la Sal** (123km/76mi ✕), where you can see the old salt pans★ by the road.

The usual way to continue beyond Gerri is through the gorge, the Estret de Collegats, to La Pobla de Segur and then along the Castelbó River to Senterada. You have that option, but we recommend taking the tiny turning to the right at the entrance to Gerri, where an inconspicuous sign says 'POBLETA DE BELLVEI'; this is magical scenery

23

(📞) all the way to **La Pobleta** (140km/87mi), on a road not even shown on some maps.

At La Pobleta, turn left for **Senterada** (144km/89mi) and then right onto the N260. You drive through desolate countryside studded with stone perched villages, up to the **Coll de Perbes** (1530m/5020ft) and then on to **Pont de Suert** (175km/109mi ⛰🏠⛺△✕🍽). Here take the N230 north back towards VIELHA. *(After 1km you have the option of a right turn to Caldes de Boí, a resort on the western fringe of the national park; allow 44km/27mi return).* The main tour continues to the **Túnel de Vielha** and back to **Vielha** itself (215km/133mi).

The Riu Escrita at Espot, en route to the entrance to the Parc Nacional d'Aigües Tortes

Car tour 7: 'GROTTES' AND GARGOYLES

Bagnères-de-Bigorre • Abbaye d'Escaladieu • Château de Mauvezin • (Esparros) • Grottes de Gargas • St-Bertrand-de-Comminges • Luchon • Col de Peyresourde • Arreau • Col d'Aspin • Bagnères-de-Bigorre

162km/100mi; about 5 hours' driving
Walks en route or nearby: 18, 19
Good surfaced roads are used throughout this tour.
Picnic suggestion: The **Col d'Aspin**, above **Arreau**, is one of

the 'high spots' of this long car tour and commands breathtaking views in all directions (note the landmark of the radio-masted Pic du Midi de Bigorre to the west).
NB: The pass can be quite exposed, and there is no shade.

To see or not to see, that will be your question, for this circuit passes the Abbey of Escaladieu, the Château de Mauvezin, the prehistoric Grottes de Gargas with their weird 'deformed-hand' imprints, the magnificent St-Bertrand-de-Comminges, the Grotte de Médous — and many beauty spots, from the Baronnies foothills to the heights of the Col d'Aspin.

Leave **Bagnères-de-Bigorrre** (🏠🏕▲△✕☎WC) on the D938, following signs for *TOULOUSE* and *CAPVERN*. At **Le Hailla** (7km/ 4.5mi) ignore the left turn to Tourney and continue to the ancient abbey★ (✝) of **Escaladieu** (13km/8mi) and then on to the **Château de Mauvezin**★ (📖🎞) on the hilltop above.
From the château descend once more towards Escaladieu and, shortly before you return to the abbey, turn left by the Auberge l'Arros (signposted 'LES BARONNIES'). Just before Bourg-de-Bigorre, cross the Arros River, following signs to the **Maison des Baronnies** (18km/11mi ▲✕WC), where the information office can supply you with full details of this great walking area, shown in the photographs on pages 90-92. Continue following the D14, ignoring turn-offs and keeping the river on your right at first. Climb to **Espèche** and then past **Lomne**, to the junction with the D26 (24km/15mi). Turn left for the **Col de Coupe** (720m/2360ft; 26km/16mi 🎞) with its views back to the velvety green and

verdant hillsides. From here a right turn would take you into the village of **Esparros** 1km away (▲; Walk 18).
At the junction with the main D929 turn right in the direction of *HECHES* and, very soon afterwards, left (just beyond a petrol station); follow the signs to '*HOSTELLERIE DE LA NESTE*'. Without actually going into Héchettes, come to a junction and turn left, continuing on the D26, through **St-Arroman** (36km/23mi). Shortly afterwards fork right (signposted '*NESTIER*'). Ignoring all turnings off the road, continue straight on through **Nestier**, to the pleasant village of **Aventignan**, just beyond which you turn right for the **Grottes de Gargas**★ (48km/30mi 🏠∩✕ WC).
Regaining the main road from the caves, turn right. **St-Bertrand-de-Comminges**★, one of the most important religious monuments in the Pyrenees (56km/35mi ✝🏛✕ WC) is soon visible on a hilltop. The tour continues via **Valcabrère** (from where you can make a short diversion to the nearby 11th-century church of St-Just★ (✝🎞)

St-Bertrand-de-Comminges

exposed, picnic spot — stop to admire the views south to the frontier peaks and ahead to the Pic du Midi de Bigorre with its peak-top observatory.

The tour now makes its final descent through forest to the wide **Plateau de Payolle** and its pleasant lake (143km/89mi ▲▲✕) and **Ste-Marie-de-Campan** (150km/93mi ♦▲▲✕♍WC), where you turn right onto the D935. The 17th-century church at **Campan** (♦▲▲△✕) and the **Grotte de Médous★** (∩), with

Arreau

and enjoy splendid views back to St-Bertrand. Some 2km beyond Valcabrère reach the N125 and turn right for **Luchon★** (also known as Bagnères-de-Luchon; 89km/ 55mi ▲▲▲△✕♍M WC). To approach Walk 19, take the D126 south for 'HOSPICE DE FRANCE'. Leave Luchon on the D618 (signposted 'COL DE PEYRESOURDE'), having first made sure that the signs are green, confirmation that the pass is open. The road climbs steeply to the precipitous village of **St-Aventin** (93km/58mi ♦) and on through **Garin** (96km/60mi ▲▲✕) to the **Col de Peyresourde** (1569m/5145ft; 108km/67mi 📷).

From the col, descend on the D618 through magnificent scenery, ignoring side-turnings, to **Arreau** (125km/78mi ▲▲▲✕♍ WC), with its attractive half-timbered buildings and covered market. Cross a bridge by the Office du Tourism, turn right onto the D929 (signposted 'COL D'ASPIN') and then almost immediately left onto the D918 (still signposted for the col). The steep 12km climb passes the lovely village of **Aspin-Aure**, a forestry community said to be one of the richest in the *département*. At the **Col d'Aspin** (📷 1489m/4885ft; 137km/85mi) — a lovely, if

their dramatic limestone formations, are the final attractions en route, before you return to **Bagnères-de-Bigorre** (162km/100mi).

Car tour 8: MARVELS AND MIRACLES

Lourdes • Bagnères-de-Bigorre • Ste-Marie-de-Campan • La Mongie • Col du Tourmalet • Barèges • Luz-St-Sauveur • Cirque de Gavarnie • (Beaucens or Cauterets) • Argelès-Gazost • Agos Vidalos • Lourdes

148km/92mi; about 4 hours' driving
Walks en route and nearby: 20-23
A comfortable circular route on good surfaced roads, starting at the famous pilgrimage town of Lourdes and including the most visited spectacle of the whole Pyrenees, the Cirque de Gavarnie.

Picnic suggestion: After parking in **Gavarnie** (WC, refreshments) follow the crowds towards the splendour of the *cirque*, passing several tables and benches set in dense woods (⌐). However, for maximum viewing pleasure continue to walk for a further 10 minutes to the **Plateau de la Prade**. There you will find a secluded spot amongst shady bushes by the stream — the young Gave du Gavarnie, which you have followed through the long valley. An alternative would be to hire the services of a pony to carry you and your picnic to the base of the *cirque*. Map page 95 (Walk 20).

Beginning and ending at the world-famous pilgrimage centre of Lourdes, this tour visits perhaps the best-known landscape in the Pyrenees — the fabulous Cirque de Gavarnie. You might also like to take the time to explore Cauterets, a mountain resort much loved by the Empress Eugénie.

Leave **Lourdes★** (✝ ▲ ▲ ✕ ➾ WC) by heading south on the N21 towards ARGELES-GAZOST, but after 3km (just before the bridge over the Gave du Pau), turn left onto the D113 to CREAC. Within minutes reach a junction and turn left (D26; signposted 'CREAC' and 'POUZAC') and continue through a gentle green landscape with its

Glacier d'Ossoue, west of Gavarnie (Walk 21)

southern backdrop of high mountains to **Pouzac** (22km/14mi). Turn right onto the D935, quickly arriving at **Bagnères-de-Bigorre** (26km/16mi 🏨🏨△✕ 🏪WC). Take the D935 south out of Bagnères, following clear overhead signs for 'LES COLS' and, after 2km, pass the wrought-iron entrance to the **Grotte de Médous★** (∩). Pass through **Campan** (32km/20mi 🍴🏨△✕) and **Ste-Marie-de-Campan** (38km/24mi 🍴🏨✕🏪WC). Almost immediately beyond Ste-Marie, turn right onto the D918, following signs for 'COL DU TOURMALET' and 'LA MONGIE'. A petrol station on the left (🏪) is your last chance to fill up before the long journey up the mountain.

From **La Mongie** (54km/34mi 🏨🏨✕) climb over towards the neighbouring resort of Barèges (together these form the biggest ski domain in the Pyrenees) via the **Col du Tourmalet** (2115m/6940ft; 58km/36mi ✕🏪WC). *(From this pass you could drive almost to the summit of the Pic du Midi de Bigorre (2872m/9420ft) on a toll-road; allow 14km/9mi return.)* The descent from the col is a spectacle of hairpin bends and high mountain scenery all the way to **Barèges** (69km/43mi 🏨🏨✕🏪WC) and **Luz-St-Sauveur★** (76km/49mi 🍴🏨🏨△✕🏪WC). Turn sharp left in the village centre onto the D921, signposted 'GAVARNIE' and, at the bridge, bear left, keeping the **Gave de Gavarnie** to the right and the elegant spa buildings of St-Sauveur on the opposite bank. As you climb beyond **Gèdre** (88km/55mi 🏨🏨✕), past the turning left to the Cirque de Troumouse (less visited than Gavarnie), the incredible **Cirque de Gavarnie★** begins to emerge, and you enjoy the view shown in the photograph on pags 96-97.

The famous 'gateway' in its rim, the Brèche de Roland (Walk 22; photograph pages 100-101), is clearly visible.

Gavarnie★ (96km/60mi 🍴🏨🏨✕ 🗼🏠WC; Walks 20-22) is just a ramshackle village of souvenir shops, but it is nevertheless the soul of the French Pyrenees and for over a century the starting-out point for the great exploits of many famous mountaineers. A short walk to the Plateau de la Prade — perhaps with a picnic — is highly recommended.

Return to Luz-St-Sauveur (116km/72mi) and, at the square, turn left following signs for ARGELES-GAZOST and LOURDES. After about 2km, turn right off the main road to **Saligos** and **Chèze**, where the statue of a giant by the sculptor Rémi Trotro outside the *poterie/créperie* menaces the valley below. Then regain the road for LOURDES; it runs through gorge-type scenery of steep cliffs, beside a wide river. Continue to **Soulom** (127km/79mi). *(Here you could take a detour to the right, to BEAUCENS, to see the birds of prey at the 'Donjon des Aigles'; allow 8km/5mi return.)* The next village en route is **Pierrefitte-Nestalas**. *(A detour to the left leads to CAUTERETS and the setting for Walk 23; 21km/13mi return.)* The main tour follows the D921 to **Argelès-Gazost** (136km/84mi 🏨🏨△✕🏪), then the N21 to **Agos Vidalos** (141km/87mi 🏨🏨✕), a village dominated on the left by the *'montagne enchantée'*, the Pic de Pibeste. The mountain's strange Mediterranean micro-climate supports the mouflon (rare wild sheep) and some plant species that are equally rare in the Pyrenees. (For information on the Pic de Pibeste, stop at the Résidence Bellevue in Agos Vidalos.) Continue on the main road back to **Lourdes** (148km/92mi).

Car tour 9: GRAND CANYONS TOUR

Torla (Parque Nacional de Ordesa) • Sarvisé • Fanlo • Buerba • Escalona • Hospital de Tella • Revilla • Bielsa • Valle de Pineta • Bielsa • Escalona • Desfiladero de Vellos (Añisclo Canyon) • Torla

215km/133mi; about 5 hours' driving
Walks en route and nearby: 24-26
A demanding drive across remote mountain wilderness and with optional visits to some of the world's most spectacular and unspoilt canyons.

Picnic suggestion: From **Torla** head north and after 3km take the track to the left through the Garganta de los Navarros that leads to Camping de Bujaruelo and then Bujaruelo. Here, along the banks of the **Ara River**, you'll find few people but possibly marmots and izards.

Visiting this incredibly beautiful region, you may wonder why it is not better known internationally. The main canyon, the Ordesa, with its kilometre-high walls, rivals America's famous Grand Canyon for spectacle.

Torla (⛺🏠△🍴) is the gateway to the fabulous **Parque Nacional de Ordesa y Monte Perdido★** and the obvious place to stay in this region. The main canyon, with its 1000m/3300ft walls, demands at the very least a day of its own (see Walk 26). For our car tour we will head south and east to take in some of the other spectacles of the area.
Head south from Torla on the A135, then N260, watching out for the breathtaking acrobatics of beautiful red kites, often seen here. Continue through **Broto** (20km/12.5mi ⛺🏠🍴🚉) and, at **Sarvisé** (23km/14mi), turn left towards FANLO.
This little road rises along the **Chate River** to almost eerie views of the desolate plateaux that top the Ordesa Canyon. **Fanlo** (32km/20mi 🏪), a once-deserted village now being renovated for holiday homes, is worth a stop for the views and the park information office.
The road now bypasses Nerin (🏪), to wind along the deepening gorge of the **Aso River**. At the next junction (39km/24mi) turn right for **Buerba**. The road climbs up to a viewpoint from which you

can see along the exquisite **Añisclo Canyon** (Walk 25), then wriggles its way spectacularly high above the **Vellos (Bellos) River** to **Puyarruego** (55km/34mi). Later we will be returning along the Vellos River, but for now turn right, and on reaching the main

La Ripareta, the idyllic picnic spot where Walk 25 in the Añisclo Canyon turns back

road (A138) at **Escalona**, turn left towards BIELSA.

On the far side of **Hospital de Tella** (66km/ 41mi), turn left, following signs for TELLA. After some 2km the road divides. Try first the upper, right-hand route, leading to **Tella** (69km/43mi 🏃) with its Hermitage of Juanipablo and the Virgen de la Peña. Then return and take the other, lower, road, on a shelf over the stunning **Yaga Canyon**. At **Revilla** (75km/47mi 📷) there is an easy 2h return walk to a look-out point ('*mirador*') signposted from the village.

Return to the A138 and continue into **Bielsa★** (92km/57mi 🛏️✕ 🚰M), a border-style shopping town. Leaving the square, follow signs for 'VALLE DE PINETA' and 'PARADOR NACIONAL MONTE PERDIDO'.

You come to the splendid **Pineta Valley**, shown on pages 106-107 (Walk 24). The *parador*

(115km/71mi ⛰️) stands at the end of the road, at the foot of the **Circo de Pineta** — a rock amphitheatre comparable to the famous French *cirques* of Gavarnie and Troumouse.

Return to **Escalona**, where you have a choice. We recommend you turn right for **Puyarruego** and then follow the road through the **Desfiladero de Vellos**, past the entrance to the Añisclo Canyon (Walk 25). The *desfiladero* is an experience you should not miss, the gorge so narrow in places that from mid-June to October a one-way system (east to west) is in operation. Once through the *desfiladero*, retrace your route to **Torla** (215km/133mi). (However, if you are in a hurry to get back to Torla, it is actually quicker to continue on straight roads — the A138 to Ainsa and then the N260 for Boltaña and Torla, saving almost 20km.)

Monte Perdido (Walk 26), the third-highest mountain in the Pyrenees and the highest limestone massif in Europe

Car tour 10: THE VALLEY OF THE BEAR

Jaca • Puente la Reina de Jaca • (Hecho • Selva de Oza) • Ansó • Col
Belagua • Arette-Pierre-St-Martin • Aspe Valley • (Lescun) •
Candanchú • Jaca

*158km/98mi; a little under 5 hours'
driving.* **Note: passports required**
Walk nearby: 27
*This tour makes the most of good
metalled roads, even in the high
mountains.*
Picnic suggestion: At the 42km-
point, instead of turning off just

before **Hecho** for Ansó, continue
straight down the fabulously
scenic Hecho Valley for
12km/7mi, until you reach the
Selva (forest) **de Oza**, a popular
recreational area with full camping
and walking facilities (🌲WC;
refreshments).

O f the score of brown bear believed still to live in the
Pyrenees, the greatest concentration is in the valleys
visited on this car tour. That is the measure of their
remoteness — but, sadly, even here the bear is under threat
and faces extinction.

Leave **Jaca** (🌲🏔🏠⛺✕🅿WC)
with its extravagant buildings,
busy shopping streets, and almost
ever-circling vultures, by taking
the N240 — the main road to
Pamplona. Almost immediately
you come upon the windswept
plains of the **Río Aragón**. After
10km/6mi pass signs to Santa
Cruz de la Serós and the famous
mountain monastery of San Juán
de la Peña (🌲). In 19km/12mi you

cross the bridge at **Puente la
Reina** (🏔✕🅿) by turning right,
following signs to 'HECHO'.
A narrow but well-surfaced road
runs through open pastureland
towards the forests and mountains
ahead. About 1km before Hecho
(42km/26mi 🏔🏠✕) take a left
turn to ANSO.* The easy and
attractive road undulates for 10km
to **Ansó** (52km/32mi 🌲🏔✕),
with its cobbled streets and
wooden balconies. Leave Ansó for
ZURIZA, keeping the river on your
left and enjoying more and more
spectacular scenery as the journey
progresses through woods of Scots
pine, fir and oak.
As the valley narrows, so the
mountains become higher and the
population, so it is said, becomes
increasingly idiosyncratic, often
wearing traditional dress (the
nearest to 'native' dress we saw

*But to see more of this beautiful
valley, follow the road through
Hecho and go on to **Siresa** with
its 9th-century monastery (🌲).
Continuing through gorge-like
scenery, you come to the popular
leisure complex of the **Selva de
Oza**. This lovely forest *(selva)* is a
very pleasant place to picnic.

31

Lescun — an optional detour of 11km return, and the starting point for Walk 27, illustrated on pages 114-117

was a farmer with an animal skin thrown over his shoulders for warmth).

As you approach the cross-country skiing resort of **Zuriza** (66km/41mi 🏔▲🗙), the gorge-like landscape opens out into a wide bowl. Just before the village, take a road to the left, climbing steeply through open hillside (📷) to a pass, where you leave Aragón and enter Navarra, before dropping down towards ISABA. At 78km/48mi come to a T-junction with the NA137 where, instead of going into Isaba to the left, you turn right for the FRENCH FRONTIER via the **Belagua Pass** (📷).

Cross the border post (102km/63mi) and enter a weird landscape of karst (limestone), eerily eroded above and penetrated below you by a labyrinth of tunnels and caves. (The caverns of Pierre-St-Martin, discovered in 1952, are amongst the deepest in the world — the entrance, just on the Spanish side, bears a memorial to speleologist Marcel Loubens who died in them.)

Leave the skiing resort of **Arette-Pierre-St-Martin** (🏔▲🗙) on the D132 (signposted 'ARETTE') and,

after 6km (108km/67mi), take the right-hand fork to the **Col de Bouezou** (114km/71mi).

Travelling through forests of huge beech trees, you come upon the pretty stone-built village of **Lées-Athas** (122km/76mi). Some 3km beyond Lées-Athas, come to the junction with the N134 (the main Vallée d'Aspe road) and turn right towards the Spanish border. *(After 2km a turning right leads to the picturesque village of Lescun; this optional detour of 11km/7mi would take you to the setting shown above and Walk 27.)*

Beyond **Urdos** (127km/79mi 🏔🗙) the road climbs through the Parc National des Pyrénées to the frontier, below which is the modern ski resort of **Candanchú** (🏔🗙) and, 9km below it, the **Canfranc** railway terminus (135km/84mi).

From here follow the valley back to **Jaca** (158km/98mi).

Brown bear

Car tour 11: LIMESTONE AND LEGENDS

St-Jean-Pied-de-Port • Col Burdincurutcheta • Col d'Orgambidesca • Larrau • Ste-Engrâce • Arette-Pierre-St-Martin • Isaba • Ochagavía • (Pamplona) • Burguete • Roncesvalles • Puerto de Ibañeta • St-Jean-Pied-de-Port

189km/117mi; about 5 hours' driving. **Note: passports required**
Walks en route and nearby: 28, 29
A long day, first visiting the gorges and startling limestone landscape of the Pic d'Anie region, then with the option of spending time in Pamplona — before returning to France via the Ibañeta Pass, scene of the legendary 'Chanson de Roland'.

Picnic suggestion: From **Roncesvalles**, continue up the hill, towards the border. After five minutes you emerge on a virtually treeless hilltop, the **Puerto de Ibañeta** (map pages 120-121), where you can park, walk and see the memorial to Roland shown on page 118. *NB: There is no shade at this pass.*

E njoy a change from the high peaks of the central Pyrenees. This tour takes you through rolling green countryside, liberally sprinkled with large white houses and well-tended farms. Luckily the roads are much easier to negotiate than the Basque language …

Leave the attractive old market town of **St-Jean-Pied-de-Port** (🏨🛏️⚠️🍴🚐WC; best access to Walk 28) in the direction of **St-Jean-le-Vieux** (4.5km/3mi), and there leave the main road by turning right onto the D18, following signs for 'STATION DE SKI D'IRATY.'
Beyond **Lecumberry** and **Mendive** (11km/7mi), the road climbs steeply through scenery at first reminiscent of the English Lake District, but soon revealing its more awesome scale at the **Col Burdincurutcheta** (1135m/ 3725ft; 24km/15mi 🚾), from where you have views towards the huge Iraty Forest ahead. Descend to a small lake, only to climb again almost immediately past Camping Iraty (⛺) to the **Col d'Orgambidesca** (1319m/4325ft; 33.5km/ 21mi 🚾), one of the most important bird migration routes in Europe and the scene of bitter confrontation between conservationists and hunters.
Descend through a series of steep hairpin bends to **Larrau**

(46.5km/29mi 🏨🛏️🍴), from where we head northeast on the D26 which runs alongside the Gave (river) de Larrau to **Laugibar** (🛏️🍴), where you could see the Crevasses d'Holçarté. Beyond Laugibar turn right (55km/34mi) onto the D113. Via the **Gorges de Kakouetta** and **Ste-Engrâce** (66km/41mi ♀) climb steeply up to the junction with the D132 and here turn right into the ski station of **Arette-Pierre-St-Martin** (76km/47mi 🏨🛏️🍴). You're amidst the spikes and spines, faults and flues of some of the most outrageous limestone scenery anywhere in the world.
Continue on the D132, the border road. Just across the frontier lies the now-barred entrance to the **Gouffre Pierre-St-Martin**, where speleologist Marcel Loubens died during the early exploration of what was then the deepest known cavern in the world. Your descent, above ground, to **Isaba** (103km/ 64mi 🏨🛏️🍴🚐) is breathtakingly beautiful. (Tour 10 follows this

33

section, but in the reverse direction.)

At Isaba take the NA140 to **Uztárroz** and **Ochagavía**, driving through a densely-forested landscape. Basque-style architecture comes into view more frequently: the huge square village and farm houses are spotlessly white-washed and roofed in slate or tiles.

At **Escároz** (124km/77mi) cross the Salazar River and turn right (signposted 'BURGUETE'). On reaching the N135 some 30km/19mi further on, decide whether to turn right with the main tour into **Burguete** (156km/97mi ▲ ✕) or left for a 90km/56mi round trip detour to Pamplona. Burguete was made famous by Hemingway in *The Sun Also Rises.*

From Burguete the road back to St-Jean-Pied-de-Port passes **Roncesvalles** (159km/99mi ✝▲✕M; Walk 29), with its unmistakable collegiate buildings and fascinating history. A little further along it climbs to the **Ibañeta Pass** (1062m/3485ft 📷), the most likely site for the massacre of Charlemagne's rearguard by the Basques in revenge for the sacking of Pamplona. The battle's inaccurate celebration in the *Chanson de Roland* is the explanation for the memorial at the pass (photograph page 118), which is also on the famous pilgrims' route to Santiago de Compostela. The pass is a good place to picnic on fine days. The road now descends to **Valcarlos** and then a further 3km to the frontier at **Arnéguy**, for the final sprint back to **St-Jean-Pied-de-Port** (189km/117mi).

Landscape in the Basque country (Car tour 12)

Car tour 12: INTO THE BASQUE COUNTRY

San Sebastián • Hernani • Goizueta • Santesteban • Elizondo • St-Etienne-de-Baïgorry • Bidarray • Pas de Roland • Ainhoa • La Rhune • St-Jean-de-Luz

205km/127mi; about 4 hours' driving; Exit 7 from the A8 motorway near San Sebastián. **Note: passports required**
Walks en route and nearby: 30-34
A full day out, beginning and ending on the coastal motorway for easy access, and visiting wild country on both sides of the border.

Picnic suggestion: Continue on the D4 from **Dantxarinea**, keeping on the French side of the border, and crossing the River Nivelle by the **Pont du Diable**. You drive through an ancient oak forest, with good parking and picnicking possibilities. You could also stretch your legs by following the GR10 to the east or west.

Although the Basque country borders the densely-populated Atlantic coastal resorts, this tour takes you quickly and easily into a region most tourists never visit. Driving is relaxing, and signposting good; you should have time to take the train up the well-known mountain landmark of La Rhune — or, better still, climb up!

From the Spanish coastal motorway near **San Sebastián★** (♦♨▲♦✕♑⊕MWC) take EXIT 7, following signs to HERNANI (♑ — fill up!). Just before **Hernani**, turn left onto the GU3410 (10km/6mi), signposted 'GOIZUETA' and 'FAGOLLAGA'. The ugly industrial development is left behind at **Ereñozu** — except for the famous El León brewery at **Pagoaga**. The road climbs steeply through densely-forested mountains to **Goizueta** (35km/22mi). Shortly before the junction at the Hotel Basa Kabi (50km/31mi ▲▲), you reach an open plateau and turn left, following signposts for 'SANTESTEBAN'.

The scenery is more pastoral now, the great forests felled for agriculture, much as on the French side of the border. Descend along the **Ezkurra River**, at one stage through a gorge, to **Santesteban** (74km/46mi ▲▲✕), where you join the N121A towards PAMPLONA (right). After 4km, turn left on the N121B to **Irurita** (♑ nearby). In Irurita again bear left, for **Elizondo** (88km/55mi ♑).

Some 3km beyond Elizondo, turn right for Errazu, thereafter climbing steeply towards the COL D'ISPEGUY and the frontier. The road cuts through wild country of moor and rock to intersect the

St-Jean-de-Luz

famous Basque landmark of the **Iparla Ridge** (Walk 30; photograph page 123) at the **Col d'Ispéguy** (☎). From the quiet frontier post, with its one or two shops, descend to **St-Etienne-de-Baïgorry** (112km/70mi 🏨🏠 ✖🍴).

Turn left along the D918 to drive the 8km to **Eyharce**, and there bear left (still D918) for **Bidarray** (126km/78mi 🏨✖; photograph page 124). *(Alternatively, some 3km beyond St-Etienne-de-Baïgorry, you could make a left turn down a tiny tarmac track signposted 'La Bastide' and follow green arrows to Bidarray, with fine views of the Iparla Ridge.)*

From Bidarray follow the main road for 12km to **Itxassou** (🏨🏠✖), turn left into the village, and from there follow signs to the **Pas de Roland★**, a curious rock formation in a gorge. According to legend, the gap was created by Roland's horse (see notes with Walks 28 and 29).

Take the D249 out of Itxassou to **Espelette** (🏨🏠✖), where you turn left towards AINHOA on the D918. After 1km (🍴 just before) turn left again into **Ainhoa** (150km/93mi 🏨✖). From here go on to the border post at **Dantxarinea** and there turn right along the **Nivelle River**. Still in France, you travel through an ancient oak wood (there are

pleasant riverside picnic spots where the road crosses the Nivelle via the **Pont du Diable**).

When you reach a T-junction, turn left (D4) to **Sare** and from there continue on the D4 for ASCAIN. Some 3km along you have the option of taking the rack railway to the top of **La Rhune★** (Larroun; 900m/2950ft; photograph page 125), the highest peak in the region, with views inland and all along the coast. Legend has it that witches used to gather on the summit.

Once in **Ascain**, follow sign-posting to nearby ST-JEAN-DE-LUZ. *(From Ascain you can also make a detour southwest to the Col d'Ibardin, a 'mini-Andorra' — do a bit of shopping or stretch your legs in the settings shown on pages 128-130: bear left on the D4 to Herboure, and from there head south on the D404. For a shorter version of Walk 32 see 'How to get there' on page 129; for Walk 33 see page 131.)**

Finally arriving at **St-Jean-de-Luz★** (176km/109mi 🏨🏠△ ✖🍴WC), you can regain the motorway, the A63. The return to JUNCTION 7, on the Spanish side of the border, brings the total distance for the circular tour to 205km/127mi. To get to Walks 31 and 32,* leave the motorway immediately before the customs, following signs for Hendaye, and then turn left under the motorway onto the D258, into Biriatou (1.4km from the motorway exit). If you're making for the Peñas de Haya* (Walk 34; photograph pages 132-133), take the N1 towards Irún.

---

*For an overview of all the walks in this area, see the map on pages 126-127.)

Country code for walkers and motorists

The experienced rambler is used to following a 'country code', but the tourist out for a lark may unwittingly cause damage, harm animals, and even endanger his own life. Do heed this advice:

- **Do not light fires.** Use camping stoves. Stub out cigarettes with care.
- **Do not frighten animals.** By making loud noises or trying to touch or photograph them, you may cause them to run in fear and be hurt.
- **Walk quietly** through all farms, hamlets and villages, **leaving gates just as you found them**. Gates do have a purpose, usually they keep animals in — or out of — an area.
- **Protect all wild and cultivated plants**. Don't try to pick wild flowers or uproot saplings. Obviously fruit and crops are someone's private property and should not be touched. Never raid anyone's wood pile.
- **Take all your litter away with you**.
- **Stay on the path** wherever it exists, to minimise damage to surrounding vegetation. Don't take short cuts on zigzag paths; this hastens ground erosion.
- **Respect local bye-laws**, especially with reference to camping *'sauvage'*. Always choose an unobtrusive site.
- **Keep well away from streams** when attending to 'calls of nature'. Do not use detergents for washing or washing-up.
- **Support** the small local shopkeepers and artisans whenever you can.
- *Special warning:* Afternoon thunderstorms are common in the Pyrenees (see 'Weather' on page 38). It can be a very frightening experience to be on an exposed mountain area when they strike. Take heed of weather reports and do ask local advice before starting off on exposed mountain walks. In thundery weather, it is always a good idea to set off very early in the day, so that you will be down off the mountainous areas by early afternoon.

Red kite. While you are in the Cauterets area (Car tour 8), you can see birds of prey, including griffon vultures and lammergiers at the Donjon des Aigles in nearby Beaucens.

☀ Walking

There are well over 400 kilometres (250 miles) of walks in this guide, the equivalent of a coast-to-coast traverse — one of the 'classics' for all serious walkers. But you don't have to be an expert walker for any of hikes we describe. None of them requires special skills (under summer conditions) and, if you are not very fit, simply turn back when you feel like it (there are short walk suggestions with most of the itineraries). Experienced and fit walkers will nevertheless find much to enjoy, for we have included some of the wildest scenery in the Pyrenees, walked pilgrim routes and World War 2 escape routes, climbed to summits (like Canigou), enjoyed the habitat of marmots, vultures and izards (the Pyrenean chamois), and not neglected the great and the famous (like the Brèche de Roland).

Weather

Walking in the mountains is very dependent on weather conditions. A walk that can be completed quickly in the early cool of a summer morning can become an endurance test in the midday heat — or positively dangerous in the afternoon, when ferocious thunderstorms frequently erupt. A walk that demands no particular skill in late summer can require special snow and ice equipment in spring — even as late as June — and may be almost impassable with the onset of autumn storms. In the high mountains of the Pyrenees there can be snow at any time of year, even in August. *Always* take local advice before setting off on walks over 2000m in summer and above 1000m in winter.

Naturally there is variation in climate. In general, the eastern and Spanish Pyrenees (excepting the Basque country) enjoy a drier Mediterranean-type climate. If the weather is bad in France, it may be better in Spain. But you don't necessarily have to go south for sun: climbing may also work, for at 1800m you may be above the clouds.

AVERAGE TEMPERATURES

	Mar-Apr	May-June	Jul-Aug	Sept-Oct
	Degrees Centigrade			
Midi-Pyrénées	7.8	17.5	20.8	18.3
Pyrénées-Roussillon	16.3	23.1	28.1	22.9
Basque Country	14.9	20.1	24.0	21.1

Transport

For non-circular itineraries we recommend getting the transport problems out of the way *before* you start the walk; if you have a car, leave it at the **destination** and take public transport to the **start** of the walk. Then you won't have to worry about missing buses or trains at the end of the day.

Clothing and equipment

Style of walking is a personal matter, and the novice will have to find his or her own. There is a minimum of equipment for safety on certain walks in this book, but remember that a law of diminishing returns is in operation. The more you carry the slower you go, so the more you need to carry. As far as clothing is concerned, flexibility is paramount; it is vital to be able to strip down to shorts and T-shirt when the going gets hot and then cover up by stages as evening approaches or as you climb (reckon on the temperature falling 1 degree Centigrade for every 100m to 200m of ascent — say every 500ft).

Time of year/weather is the most important factor to consider, when you're planning what equipment to take. The Brèche de Roland, for example (one of the most famous goals for walkers in the Pyrenees), is at its easiest when snow covers the glacier in early autumn or late spring — at the height of summer, only the most determined will get up the naked ice without benefit of crampons. But that is an exception to the rule that, the harsher the weather, the more you will have to carry.

Total distance, metres of ascent, availability of supplies, and the existence of 'escape routes' (quick ways back to safety) are other factors. Below we give a checklist of equipment you *might* take: you will have to use your own judgement about what is right for you.

Backpack or small rucksack
Stove and fuel
Sunhat
Warm hat
Torch or headlamp
Waterproof trousers
Survival bag
  (in case of accident)
First aid kit
Sleeping bag or sheet
  (for refuges)
Bivvi sac or lightweight tent
  (for sleeping out)
Fleece
Windcheater (zip opening)

Compass, GPS
Matches
Sunglasses and suncream
Gloves
Gaiters
Waterproofs
Large-scale map
  1:25,000 or 1:50,000
Food and water
Rope
Crampons
Ice axe
Warm undergarments
Mobile phone (the **emergency**
  number is 112)

Food and water

Some of the itineraries described visit mountain refuges where meals can be obtained *(**always** telephone in advance to confirm that they are open, even in summer)*, but usually you will have to carry food with you. The correct amount of food for you is something that can only be discovered by experience, but remember that food is fuel and, when you are running down at the end of the day, a fast-energy food can give you a terrific boost.

Water is even more vital, but we often find it impossible to carry enough. In the high mountains of the Pyrenees it is safe to drink from streams, provided there is no habitation above you (mountain villages invariably flush toilets directly into streams). Check your map and, provided that no possible source of pollution is shown, and the stream is vigorous, then there is no problem — you'll be enjoying 'mineral' water — free!

Waymarking, maps, and grading of the walks

Some of the walks in this book incorporate sections of GR routes (in French, 'Grande Randonnée'; in Spanish 'Senderos de Gran Recorrido'). These GR routes have a special system of waymarking, explained below. Other walks incorporate sections of local walking itineraries, which may have other systems of waymarking. Finally there are walks that are not marked in any way and for which you will have to rely entirely upon the descriptions and maps in this book.

Grande Randonnée (GR) waymarking

This system uses red and white paint stripes — on trees, rocks, and walls (even on the ground), to indicate the route. On difficult sections the marks tend to be quite close together; on easy sections, with little chance of getting lost, they may be more widely spaced. Where such GR waymarking is significant along the route of our walks, we refer to it: thus, if you walk for more than a few minutes without seeing a red and white mark, you have come off the GR route. The next important thing to remember is that an X with one stroke in red and the other in white means 'Wrong Way'. A slash through the stripes means 'Diversion'. An arrow with the stripes means 'Change of Direction'.

Maps

The maps in this book should be sufficient for all the walks you plan using this guide — enough for a holiday of four weeks' walking every day. And you will save a great deal of money, since you would need almost twenty large-scale maps to cover walking routes throughout the range. Nevertheless, many readers may wish to purchase some good large-scale maps, showing all the GR routes and overnight hostels.

Rando Editions (together with various partners) publishes maps for the entire Pyrenees at a scale of 1:50,000, providing sufficient detail for most purposes. In many cases these maps cover both the **French** and **Spanish** sides of the range on a single sheet. However, if you require more detail, there are 1:25,000 IGN maps for the **French Pyrenees** and **Andorra** (the 'TOP 25' Series). Some parts of the **Spanish Pyrenees** are also covered by the 1:40,000 maps published by Editorial Alpina.

The maps mentioned above may be purchased in the Pyrenees or from your local map stockist.

Grading of the walks

Note that the distances quoted are calculated from the map. On steep terrain they may be considerable underestimates, as maps cannot show all of the hairpins that actually exist.

Easy: good surface; limited ascent; no technical skill or special equipment required; may still be long.

Moderate: changeable surface; usually a steep ascent/descent; the walk may be very long.

Difficult: may involve any or all of the following: scrambling over difficult surfaces; steep ascents/descents; poor sign-posting. Suitable walking equipment required.

Safety and guides

Safe walking in the mountains is a matter of judgement, just like driving a car or crossing a road. And that judgement cannot easily be taught in books; it has to be acquired, preferably by going with other experienced walkers. If you are a novice, begin with some of the lower, shorter walks, take it easy, and build from there.

Much is made of the dangers of walking alone, but also it can be dangerous to be the slowest and weakest member of an aggressive party. (It also causes no end of worry to set off in a group and then split up with the intention of somehow meeting again later.) *Judgement!* In season, on popular routes, the solo walker in trouble will find help near at hand; out of season, or in more remote parts, self-help (and that implies two or more people) is the only solution.

Should you wish to hire a **guide** for any walks in the region, enquire at the nearest *Syndicat d'initiative* (tourist information office).

Organisation of the walks

There are 34 main walks in this book, spread across the entire Pyrenees (France, Spain and Andorra). Many are accessible by public tansport, but for the more remote parts of the range the use of a car is essential. Ten walks are in the eastern Pyrenees and easily reached from the Costa Brava or Côte Vermeille; seven are in the western Pyrenees, for those based at resorts like Biarritz or San Sebastián; the remainder are spread among the high peaks between Andorra and the Pic d'Anie. Several walks cross the frontier, so have your passport with you (but there will only be an izard to look at it). For those with a little time, *all* the walks are accessible, since the chain is only 400km coast-to-coast, with an excellent motorway and railway system.

Begin by taking a look at the fold-out map and noting the walks that are nearest to you. Then turn to the route notes and the accompanying large-scale maps. Each walk is described in the direction we think the most attractive and that poses the least transport problems, but you may prefer the reverse direction. To help you get the 'feel' of the walk, there is at least one photograph for each.

Every itinerary begins with planning information — distance, grade, how to get to and from the walk, etc. Pay particular attention if we refer to an ascent — 1000 metres is pretty tough going for the average walker. Times are given for reaching certain points in the walk, but bear in mind that everyone walks at a different speed … and that personal speeds will vary according to the load carried, the weather, and the time of day. As a rule of thumb, reckon on 4km/h on a good track on the flat and add one hour for every 300m/1000ft of ascent. *No time is included for stops;* increase the times by *at least* one-third to allow for lunch stops, photographs and nature-watching.

These symbols are used on the walking maps:

═══	motorway	◆▸	spring, waterfall, etc	■	specific building
━━━	main road	✚✚	church.chapel	⌷	watchtower
───	secondary road	†	shrine or cross	∩	cave
▒▒▒	minor or untarred road	⊞	cemetery	✕	quarry, mine
─── ‥‥	track.path or trail	⌂P	picnic place	🏛	stadium
╍╍ 2→	main walk	👓	best views	△	campsite
╍╍ 2→	alternative	🚌	bus stop	📖	map continuation
─ ‥ ─	park boundary	🚗	car parking	⋮	danger!
─ ‥ ─	national boundary	🚂	railway station	⅂⌐	prehistoric site
─ 400 ─	height in metres	⏛	ferry	⏦	power station
⟍	ski lift	■	castle, fort	◮	rock formation

Overnight accommodation

There are mountain *refuges* along some of our itineraries, offering refreshments, meals and very simple accommodation, usually in dormitories. None of the walks requires an overnight stop but, if you do stay overnight (for instance at the Refugio Góriz (Walk 26) or at Sarradets (Walk 22), then obviously you will have more time to enjoy the scenery and make side-trips. If you plan to spend a night at a refuge, it is preferable to take a sleeping bag, or at least a sleeping-bag liner — the blankets are a little unsavoury. *Always telephone ahead to make sure that the* refuge *is open, even in high summer.* And make sure that there are enough places — in high season the *refuges* can be a nightmare of recumbent bodies on floors and in corridors.

The French *gîte d'étape* is one grade above a refuge, but these are normally located in a hamlet or village on the valley floor, rather than on a mountaintop. *Gîtes* are good bases for those seeking budget accommodation and perhaps the *camaraderie* of fellow walkers and climbers.

Lightweight **camping** is generally possible in the high mountains, but note that some local authorities prohibit it. In the Spanish national parks (Aigües Tortes and Ordesa), bivouacs are only permitted at official sites; in the Parc National des Pyrénées (France), bivouacs must be at least 1km away from the roads.

Language hints

Throughout this book, names of places are given in the form in which they are most commonly seen locally and on walking maps (generally French names in France, Spanish names for most of the Spanish Pyrenees — but occasionally the Basque or Catalan form). Expect to see many variations — on maps, in guides, and on signposting! A short glossary of place name meanings is on page 44.

In case you become lost, you may have to ask the way. Here's one way to ask directions and understand the answers you get! First, memorise the few 'key' and 'secondary' questions shown overleaf. **Then, always follow up your key question with a second question demanding a yes or no answer.** Following are the two most likely situations in which you will have to practice your French or Spanish. The dots (…) show where you will fill in the name of your destination. We assume that you are familiar with the basics of French and Spanish pronunciation, but it's a good idea to ask a local person to help you with the pronunciation of place names.

Asking the way

The key questions

English	French	Spanish
Hallo.	Bonjour.	Buenos días.
I am lost.	Je me suis perdu.	Me he extraviado.
Please —	S'il vous plaît —	Por favor —
Where is	Où se trouve	Dónde está
the road to … ?	la route de … ?	la carretera a … ?
the path to … ?	le sentier de … ?	la senda de … ?
the bus stop?	l'arrêt d'autocar?	la parada?
the station?	la gare?	la estación?

Secondary questions leading to a yes/no answer

Is it here?	Est-ce (que c'est) ici?	Está aquí?
there?	là-bas?	allá?
straight ahead?	tout droit?	todo recto?
behind?	derrière?	detrás?
to the left?	à gauche?	a la izquierda?
to the right?	à droite?	a la derecha?
above?	en haut?	arriba?
below?	en bas?	abajo?
Thank you.	Merci.	Gracias.

Asking a taxi driver to take you somewhere and return for you, or asking a taxi driver to collect you somewhere:

English	French	Spanish
Please —	S'il vous plaît —	Por favor —
Take us to …	Emmenez-nous à …	Llévanos a …
Come and pick us	Venez nous chercher	Venga buscarnos
up at … (place)	à …	a …
at … (time) *	à … *	a … *

Instead of memorizing the hours of the day, simply point out on your watch the time you wish to be collected, or write it down.

Place name meanings (B: Basque; P: used throughout the Pyrenees)

ague, aigüe — water (P)	*erreka* — stream (B)
aran — valley (B)	*etehola* — hut (B)
arri — stone (B)	*farga* — ancient forge (P)
barranc, barranco — ravine (P)	*font* — spring (P)
bide — path (B)	*gave* — mountain torrent (P)
borda — farmhouse (B)	*hourguette* — steep pass (P)
borde — farm (P)	*iban* — valley (B)
campana — rock 'needle' (P)	*jasse* — level pasture (P)
celhay — plateau (B)	*marcadau* — market (P)
chipi — small (B)	*mendi* — mountain (B)
col, coll, collado — pass (P)	*orri, orrhy* — stone hut (P)
cortal — shepherd's hut (P)	*pené* — ridge (P)
coume — narrow valley (P)	*prat* — meadow (P)
cuby — bridge (B)	*río, riu* — river (P)
estany — pond, lake (P)	*val* — valley (P)
étang — pond (P)	*zubi* — bridge (B)

Walk 1: VILAJUÏGA • DOLMEN DE LA VINYA DEL REI • SANT PERE DE RODES • SERRA DE L'ESTELA • LLANÇÀ

Distance: 16km/10mi; 4h
Grade: moderate — involves some 700m/2300ft of ascent
Equipment: Vegetation is prickly, so keep legs covered; strong footwear, water, picnic, swimming gear; compass an advantage
How to get there: 🚂 (RENFE 902 24 34 02; www.renfe.com) or 🚌 (SARFA 902 302 025; www.sarfa.com) to Vilajuïga. Or 🚗 (Car tour 1; park at Vilajuïga station).

To return: 🚂 from Llançà to Vilajuïga (RENFE, as above)
Short walk: Walk only as far as **Dolmen de la Carena**, returning by the same route or along the road (2h return; easy climb of some 200m/650ft).
Alternative walk: Holidaymakers staying in Llança can follow the last GR11 section of the walk backwards to **Sant Pere de Rodes**, returning to Llança by the same route (3h return).

This walk has everything — magnificent scenery, prehistoric remains, an important Romanesque monastery, a ruined castle, and a swim in the Mediterranean to cool off at the end of the hike.

From **Vilajuïga** STATION, **start out** by walking under the bypass road and keeping straight on along the old main road (Carretera de Roses), from where you have a clear view of Quermanço Castle. Then take the second left into the village. In the first square, PLAÇA MARGINEDA, there is an ancient synagogue (incorporated into Sant Feliu). Continue past AIGUES MINERALS DE VILAJUIGA (where, Mondays to Fridays, you can fill your water bottle at the spring) and turn right, following the road signposted 'ST PERE DE RODES'. Some 0.8km beyond the last

house, where a large panel announces 'CAP DE CREUS, PARC NATURAL' take the earthen track to the right, clearly signposted, 'DOLMENS' (**30min**).

Marked occasionally by YELLOW PAINT FLASHES (local footpath waymarking), the track starts out with an olive grove to the left, then runs between a stream bed and another olive grove, after nine minutes (**39min**) becoming impassable to vehicles. Continue on a clearly-defined path for another eight minutes (**47min**) — to where another STREAM BED JOINS FROM THE LEFT. Cross the

The first written reference to the beautiful monastery of Sant Pere de Rodes dates from the 9th century, but the restoration of the buildings has caused controversy.

(normally dry) stream bed you have been following, to get onto an ascending path that keeps the new stream bed immediately to its left. After two minutes (**49min**) the path divides: go left and cross the new stream bed (there's a yellow paint flash to make it clear). In three minutes (**52min**) you will be at your first *dolmen*, the **Vinya del Rei** (**1** on the map), a stone burial chamber dating from approximately 5000 years ago. Having found your first *dolmen*, the next four are easy — roughly in line as you ascend the spine of the hill. In **56min**, come to **Dolmen del Garrollar** (to the right of the path; **2**), then **La Talaia** (**3**; **1h**), **Les Ruïnes** (**4**; **1h01min**) and **La Carena** (**5**; **1h04min**). Continue climbing beyond La Carena and, in **1h09min**, you arrive on the tarmac road from Vilajuïga. Turn right along the road and in 40 paces come to a sign, 'COVA DEL LLOP CAIGUTS I & II'. If you take the path which plunges into the scrub, you can see these *dolmen* (**6** and **7**) and be back on the road again in 15 minutes (**1h25min**). Six minutes further on (**1h31min**) another path to the right takes in

Vinyes Mortes I (**8**) and II (**9**). Return to the road (**1h41min**) and continue for a further 10 minutes — to where a dirt track signposted 'MAS MARGALL' turns off to the left.

Follow the track to the ruined farm of **Mas Margall** (**1h53min**), where you take the fork to the right, climbing above the *mas*. In another minute, where your track joins another, turn left. At the next divide, fork right and in 10 minutes cross the tarmac road and take the track directly opposite, signposted 'SANT ONOFRE'. In a hundred paces, your onward route, signposted 'SANTA HELENA, ST PERE DE RODES' is to the left; but first, if you like organised picnic spots, there are tables and benches under the pines at **Mas Ventós**, two minutes straight ahead (**2h05min**).

Continuing, the well-trodden path climbs up to the **Serra de Santa Helena**, giving the opportunity to visit the ruined castle of **Sant Salvador de Verdera**, the controversially restored monastery of **Sant Pere de Rodes**, and the church of **Santa Helena** (best in that order). From Santa Helena, follow the path northwards that

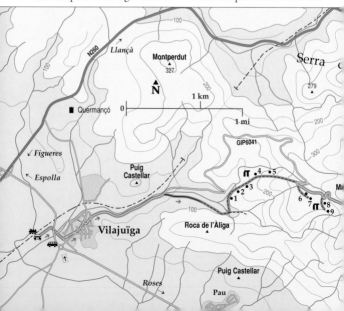

descends to the road, continue northwards and, just after the junction signposted 'PORT DE LA SELVA', take the track signposted 'COLL PERER, LLANÇA' (**2h40min** — not including sightseeing). This is also the GR11 and is marked with red and white stripes. The track descends only slightly at first, northwards, but after eight minutes it begins to swing more to

Many farms are now in ruins.

the right (northeast). After 15 minutes on this track, you pass a RUINED BARN about 200m/yds away to your right (**2h56min**) and continue up the hill towards a low RADIO MAST. The track curves to the left and then, quite unexpectedly, the red and white stripes direct you off the track, to the right (**3h**), along a much poorer path and over the SADDLE of the hill. From the saddle you descend eastwards. You drop down to a stone-built shepherd's '*orri*', almost concealed by vegetation, climb a little and then descend steeply into a low point, the **Coll del Perer** (**3h10min**), a good area to spot red-legged partridges.

Ignore the path that climbs the hill straight ahead, as well as the one to the right that heads towards La Vall de Santa Creu, and instead turn left (north) along a gully. Some five minutes from the dip, come to a look-out point (**3h15min**) which makes a convenient place to take a break. Ahead of you are the church and white houses of Llançà, the higher Pyrenees (the Albères), the coast stretching away to the border, and an ugly quarry.

Continue on a clear path which descends to the little stream known as the **Rec d'en Prim** (dry in summer) and meander along until you reach the new Les Esplanes area of **Llançà** at a large ROUNDABOUT (**3h45min**). From here take CARRER SANT PERE DE RODA, and make your way to the PLAÇA MAJOR (you'll see the church tower sticking up above the surrounding buildings). Here you can get a well-deserved drink and a taxi. To swim, walk down to the sea; for a train, leave the square in the direction of the main road and then cross the road to get to the STATION (**4h**).

Walk 2: (ROSES) • CADAQUES • CALA JONCOLS • ROSES

Distance: 20km/12.5mi; 6h15min
Grade: quite easy (the walk undulates between sea level and 300m/985ft); GR92 waymarking
Equipment: sturdy shoes, water, picnic, swimming gear
How to get there and return: This walk begins with a 🚢 ferry ride from Roses, reached by 🚌 (SARFA 902 30 20 25, www.sarfa.com; SAGALES 902 13 00 14, www.sagales.com; or Alsina Graells 902 42 22 42, www.alsa.es). Or 🚗: park inside the harbour at Roses. Take the 🚢 ferry (609 328 177) from the harbour to Cadaqués.

Short walk: Take the ferry from Roses as far as either **Cala Jóncols** or **Cala Montjoi** *(making clear that you wish to disembark there)* and walk back. The section from Cala Montjoi to the *zona militar* is especially beautiful.
Alternative walk: Holidaymakers staying in Cadaqués may wish to do the walk in reverse, taking the ferry to Roses and walking back.
Other useful contacts: taxi 972 25 47 49 or 972 25 30 33; Roses Tourist Office 972 25 73 31, www.roses.net; Cadaques Tourist Office 972 25 83 15, www.costabrava guide.com

Cadaqués, made famous by the surrealist artist Salvador Dalí, who lived nearby, effortlessly combines bohemianism and sophistication. For this memorable day out, take the ferry to Cadaqués from the harbour at Roses and then walk back, pausing to swim along the way.

Begin the walk on the PASSEIG in **Cadaqués**, a cool, tree-lined square close to where the ferries dock. Follow the sea-front road southwards (right, as you face the sea) along RIBA NEMESI LLORENS, through the PLAÇA DR PONT, and then via RIBA PIXOT and CARRERA DEL DR BARTUMEUS/CARRETERA DE ROSES A CADAQUES). You pass the Hotel Llane Petit and come to the ROCAMAR HOTEL.
By the Rocamar there is a choice of three routes: ignore the surfaced road to the left (which leads into the hotel grounds) and

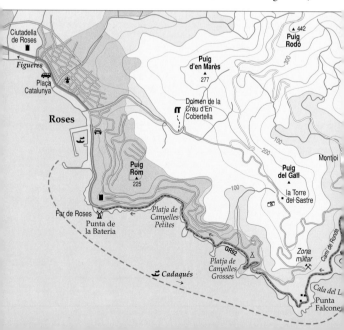

Top: landscape east of Roses in late spring; above: Dolmen de la Creu d'en Cobertella

ignore, too, the track ahead. Instead, take the track to the right and follow the GR waymarks to climb past a house named 'ELIANE' and cut some bends off the track. Soon the route emerges into open country. After about **25min** the track divides. Go right, climbing over a rock-slab surface and heading inland — the aim is to take a short cut across the peninsula, not to follow the coast.

After another 25 minutes pass an isolated whitewashed house with blue shutters (MAS D'EN BALTRE) and, almost immediately, cross a STONE BRIDGE (**50min**). At the divide beyond it, ignore the more tempting left-hand track. Go right instead, ascending on a poor surface (an orange sign painted on a rock advertises apartments at Cala Jóncols). As you climb, the Faro (lighthouse) de Cala Nans becomes briefly visible away to the left.

In **1h15min** ignore a track to the right (which goes towards Puig el Pení, with its unmistakable radar globes), and continue past a well-fenced house — to a high point where the track divides (**1h40min**). Go right (the left fork is a private track to a house). As the views open out, you will see, far ahead, a track winding southwards; this is your onward route to Roses. Moments later, Cala Jóncols (possibly your first appointment with a swimming costume) appears far below. Deteriorating to become impassable to anything but the most rugged jeep, the track descends to a junction with the TRACK FROM ROSES (**2h40min**). Turn left and in 20 minutes (**3h**) arrive at the beach and hotel at Cala Jóncols. It's hard to know what to do first, drink or swim.

When you are ready to continue the walk, climb the stone steps at the far end of the beach, and then turn left onto a path which heads southeast. Five minutes from the beach (**3h05min**, not including stops), bear right towards the SADDLE and, once on the saddle, bear right again. The path now descends to a stream (dry in summer) and then climbs to the landward end of the **Cap de Norfeu**, where you regain the track (**3h12min**). Ignore the track off left partway along the peninsula (but you'll get some fine views there if you have the energy) and continue on down to swim at **Cala Montjoi** (**4h15min**).

Now, from the far end of the beach, follow the footpath signed 'CAMI DE RONDA' (also the GR92 footpath, occasionally marked by red and white stripes). The route passes the famous El Bulli restaurant, a tiny cove (**4h17min**), and **Cala Rostella** (**4h31min**) — to bring you into **Cala Murtra** (**4h43min**), a naturist beach (do you dare?). Here be sure to cross the GULLY before looking for the path onwards, which climbs very steeply.

When you reach the abandoned bunkers in the *zona militar* at **Punta Falconera** (**5h**), turn left onto a track and almost immediately left again on a path that heads for an old METAL LOOKOUT TOWER and then continues to follow the coast, eventually joining tarmac (**5h14min**).

You are now back in civilisation, but the coastal path will continue to delight. Soon you can descend steps from the road to Almadrava Beach (also known as **Canyelles Grosses**; **5h17min**), from where the path continues beside the sea to the fine sand beach of **Canyelles Petites** (**5h35min**) and then to the **Far de Roses** (lighthouse; **5h 57min**), from where you are obliged to follow the road back to the harbour at **Roses** (**6h15min**).

Walk 3: COLLIOURE • NOTRE-DAME-DE-CONSOLATION • TOUR MADELOC • BANYULS-SUR-MER

See also photograph page 13
Distance: 13km/8mi; 4h15min
Grade: easy underfoot — but involves 600m/1970ft of ascent
Equipment: sturdy shoes, picnic, water
How to get there: 🚌 (Courriers Catalans 04 68 55 68 00 or www. courrierscatalans.com) or 🚆 (SNCF 08 36 35 35 35/freephone within France 08 05 90 36 35 or www.sncf.com) to Collioure; or 🚗 (Car tour 1; park at Collioure, by the harbour).
To return: 🚌 or 🚆 from Banyuls-sur-Mer
Short walk: Follow the main walk to **Notre-Dame-de-Consolation** and return the same way (1h; easier ascent of 150m/490ft).

Here's a glorious high-level walk between two Côte Vermeille resorts with artistic claims to fame. Collioure was once the much-favoured summer haunt of the group of radical artists known as the Fauves ('wild beasts') because of their use of vivid and emotive colour and form. Among the more well-known members of the school were Matisse, Derain, Vlaminck and Rouault. Banyuls-sur-Mer was the birthplace and long-time home of world-famous sculptor Aristide Maillol.

Start out at **Collioure** by following the RUE DE LA REPUBLIQUE up from the harbour to the busy main road. Notice straight ahead, on the skyline, the Tour Madeloc, the highest point of the walk. Cross the main road and, almost directly opposite, take the RUE DU TEMPLE, passing under the RAILWAY LINE into the RUE DE LA GALERE and then the RUE DE LA CONSOLATION. The way is marked by discreet YELLOW PAINT FLASHES.
At **14min**, at a fork, take the narrow road to the left signposted 'CONSOLATION'. The road climbs gently through vineyards to the bypass flyover. Carry on under the FLYOVER, keeping the stream to your left initially, but at **22min** crossing a little BRIDGE to the opposite side. Just beyond the bridge take the left-hand fork and, a moment later, on the right, the distinctively cobbled old pilgrimage trail, marked 'ERMITAGE BAR/HOTEL'. The path, later concreted, climbs steeply to the SHRINE OF 'STE-ANNE' (**27min**), beyond which descend the tarmac

View on the climb to the Tour Madeloc over vineyards and Banyuls

road. Just before a sharp bend (**30min**), take the stone steps on the left and, then, the little path that leads to the old hermitage of **Notre-Dame-de-Consolation**, now a hotel and restaurant, where you may wish to pause for a drink.

To continue, ignore the clear, wide path ahead; instead, ascend a few steps on the left and pass behind a derelict building. After a steep, rocky climb, reach a *RIDGE* (**40min**) and ascend to the right (south).

The well-marked path now runs amongst low scratchy bushes, climbing gently before zigzagging up to a wide tarmac road (D86; **1h05min**). Turn right for about 500 paces, until you come to a long bend with low bollards; there take a track running obliquely to the left, marked with *YELLOW FLASHES*.

Climb to a saddle and ascend the steep ridge towards the **Batterie de Taillefer** which soon comes into view and is reached after **1h45min**. Beyond this battery,

the track merges in four minutes
with another coming up from the
left. Almost immediately, leave
this vehicle track and take the well-
maintained path to the right; it
climbs gradually.

At **2h10min** an old watchtower
comes into view and the path
zigzags sharply up to it through
some hairpin bends. The **Tour
Madeloc** (**2h20min**) was built by
James I of Mallorca at the end of
the 13th century as part of a
lookout/communication system.
While the tower is closed to the

public, the spectacular views
remain — all along the Côte
Vermeille and the Costa Brava,
inland to the Col de Banyuls, and
to another tower further west, the
Tour de la Massane.

From the Tour Madeloc descend
on a narrow tarmac road to
another BATTERY (**2h40min**). Just
beyond the main gates, take the
narrow footpath marked with
BLUE AND WHITE FLASHES. You
drop down steeply towards
Banyuls-sur-Mer, which you can
see on the coast.

Maillol's La Pensée, *at his tomb near Banyuls*

At **2h45min** meet a path coming from the right. This is the famous GR10, here combined with the more demanding Haute Route Pyrénées (HRP), the final leg of an adventure that for some will have begun over 400km away — at Hendaye on the Atlantic coast. You will be following this path, marked clearly with RED AND WHITE FLASHES, down to the coast. At **2h50min** a vehicle track, also marked with red and white flashes, joins from the right, and you emerge on tarmac (again the D86, the 'Circuit de Vignoble' — route of the vineyards).

Turn right along the road for not more than about 30 seconds; then take a clear red-and-white-marked path on the left, short-cutting hairpin bends, to regain tarmac and reach a *table d'orientation* (**3h05min**). Beyond it, the road sweeps round to the right in a hairpin bend, but you continue straight ahead — on the right-hand, slightly higher of two earthen tracks. From here on the number of side-turnings is too great to show on the map or describe. Carefully follow the well-marked but convoluted GR on its descending course, at **3h40min** meeting a surfaced road. Turn left

and, almost immediately, right. Very soon bear right onto an unmade vehicle track along a low ridge until, at **3h50min**, you reach a house with a 2m/6ft-high wire fence. Here you will see your path running between the vineyards. Descend towards the RAILWAY LINE and pass through a TUNNEL underneath it (**4h**). Cross a main road at a T-junction and follow a concrete path between high walls.

You reach the AVENUE PUIG DEL MAS, one of the main streets in **Banyuls-sur-Mer**, at **4h05min**. Turn left to the beach. Just before reaching the sea front, look out for a plaque on the building (now a shoe shop) where the sculptor Maillol was born. The BUS STOP is on the seafront (**4h15min**), as is the taxi rank, while the railway station is close by and clearly signposted *'gare'*. If you have the time, be sure to visit the Musée Maillol and the artist's tomb (*'tombeau'*) on the outskirts of town.

Walk 4: FAGEDA D'EN JORDA • SANTA PAU • VOLCA DE SANTA MARGARIDA • VOLCA CROSCAT • FAGEDA D'EN JORDA

Distance: 15km/9.5mi; 3h45min
Grade: easy, except for the fairly steep climb of 200m/650ft to the rim of the Santa Margarida crater
Equipment: sturdy shoes, water, picnic
How to get there and return:
🚌 to Olot from Figueres (TEISA 972 20 48 68 or www.teisa-bus.com); then 🚕 taxi (972 26 15 66) to Can Serra, the parking area for the Fageda d'en Jordà; pre-arrange your return. Or 🚗 to Can Serra (Car tour 2; about 3.5km south-east of Olot on the GI524).

Short walk: Omit Santa Pau; continue directly to **Volcà de Santa Margarida** and **Volcà Croscat**, saving 1h30min. (Be sure to visit Santa Pau by car afterwards.)
Other useful numbers: Olot Tourist Office: 972 26 01 41, www.turismeolot.com; Park information: 972 26 60 12, http://mediambient.gencat.net and follow links for Fageda d'en Jorda; Museu dels Volcans: 972 26 67 62, www.olot.cat/cultura; www.turismegarrotxa.com

Behind the Costa Brava lies one of the most important volcanic regions in Europe, the Garrotxa. The earliest eruption was some 350,000 years ago, the most recent 11,500 years ago. Our walk takes you first through the Fageda d'en Jordà, a once-great beech wood, into this strange volcanic region which, with its curious light and lush vegetation, has long inspired artists such as Joaquim Vayreda, one of the founders of the Olot School.

Start out at **Can Serra**. Cross the road and follow a clear path into the **Fageda d'en Jordà**. In summer you will be grateful for the shade of these marvellous trees. In **2min** reach a signpost. We are going to follow Circuit 1 of the PNZVG (natural park) as far as 'VOLCA STA MARGARIDA'.

Meander through the wood, following the signs, and in **16min** join a tarmac road. Turn right. In two minutes more (**18min**) pick up the red and white paint flashes of the GR2 and follow the road past the **Cooperativa La Fageda**, to the beautiful old stone farmhouse shown overleaf (**Prat de la**

Left, top to bottom: the little church of Sant Miquel Sacot; Prat de la Plaça, an old stone farmhouse; the ermita in the floor of the Volcà de Santa Margarida. Below: the beeches of the Fageda d'en Jordà. Bottom: in the Volcà Croscat (an easy detour on the return route)

Plaça, 28min). Turn left on a track which runs along the side of the house, and one minute further on, leave the track, taking a path to the right. Climb steadily over mud and steep rock, and finally through a gully between fields, to emerge on the brow of a hill overlooking the little church of **Sant Miquel Sacot** (**40min**). Beyond it is the tree-clad cone of Santa Margarida.

Descend to the CHURCH on tarmac, and from there follow the sign indicating 'VOLCA STA MARGA-RIDA'. Your path passes to the right of the church. Almost immediately, take a rough path to the right, descending steeply. At the bottom of the hill you emerge onto track again (**45min**); turn right and within moments come to a junction, where you turn right again and pass a SHRINE. After a further couple of minutes come to a major junction of tracks. Ignore those to left and right and see ahead two possibilities: choose the left-hand track which has the appearance of (and sometimes is) the route of a motorcycle scramble. At the top of this ascent (**50min**) cross a good track and take a lesser one, to continue in the same direction. Pass a 3m/10ft-high 'cliff' of eroded ash, an indication that you are now ascending the cone of Margarida. By **57min** follow signs for 'S. MARGARIDA 15MIN, S. PAU 30MIN'. After another minute, a sign directs you left to the cone of Margarida. In **1h** the track divides. For now ignore the crater (up to the left) and continue ahead for Santa Pau, skirting a FARM (**1h05min**), and joining a track where a sign soon directs you to the left for SANTA PAU. In 40 minutes you can be enjoying the medieval centre of **Santa Pau** (**1h45min**) and a drink in one of the cafés.

Refreshed, retrace your steps back to the signposted junction you reached 1h into the walk and climb the zigzag path through dense forest to the RIM of the **Volcà de Santa Margarida**. Then descend to the *ermita* shown opposite (**2h45min**). Relax, the last eruption in the area was 11,500 years ago (...on the other hand, experts have deduced that the cycle of activity is 10,000 years!).

Climb back to the rim of the crater and take the clearly signposted path for 'VOLCA CROSCAT'. This descends the north side of the cone, crosses the road to the RESTAURANT SANTA MARGARIDA, and passes around the north side of **Volcà Croscat**. You are now back on PNZVG Circuit 1: follow signs to 'FAGEDA D'EN JORDA', to regain the large **Can Serra** CAR PARK in one hour (**3h45min**).

If you have the time, once back in Olot, visit the Casal dels Volcans, which explains the geology of the region, and the Museu Comarcal, which features the work of many of the artists it has inspired.

Walk 5: SANT ANIOL D'AGUJA

See also photograph page 62
Distance: 9km/5.5mi; 3h
Grade: moderate, with an ascent of about 500m/1650ft; some slippery sections and river crossings
Equipment: no special equipment, but be prepared for wet feet. See notes on 'Walking', page 38.
How to get there and return:
🚌 (Car tour 2): just east of Castellfollit de la Roca take the road GIP5233 for Montagut and Sadernes, crossing the Pont (bridge) de Plansarenes. The tarmac turns to dirt track in the hamlet of Sadernes, where there is a car park on the left (in front of the church, below the restaurant). You should continue along the track, however, following signs for

'Sant Aniol', to the last of a series of small car parks. From here a chained-off track, signposted 'Sant Aniol' descends to the river. *Note:* On weekends and throughout high season, vehicle access to the track beyond Sadernes may not be possible between 9am and 5.30pm. In this case you will have to use the car park in front of the church (3.6km/2.2mi; 55min from the start of the walk). The track walk from Sadernes to the walk start proper is beautiful, with some great views, but be sure to increase walking times accordingly! Our advice is to avoid weekends and arrive early.
Short walk: to **Sant Aniol** and return by the same path (2h)

A n astonishing lesson in social history. As you enjoy your holiday trek, not hard but invigorating, you are following the traditional everyday routes of country folk, past a chapel and through villages now long deserted.

We start our timings from the most northerly CAR PARKING AREA, where a chain prevents all but authorised vehicles descending the track to the river (signposted 'SANT ANIOL'). As you descend this track — and throughout almost the entire walk — loose stones are a menace, and care should be taken, especially on downhill sections. In **6min** cross the **Riera** (river) **de Sant Aniol**. It may be dry at this point, or you may have to use stepping stones — or even take off your boots and paddle (depending on the season). Almost immediately afterwards, there *may* be a sign pointing to 'TALAIXA', up a track to the left. But you continue *straight ahead*, until you are surrounded by the open fields of the farm of **La Muntada** (**20min**). Leave the track (which crosses the river) and continue straight ahead on a narrow path which in two minutes brings you to a little WEIR (**22min**). Pick your

way across the top of the wall. You are now entering the dramatic canyon section of the walk. The path hugs the left bank of the stream (ie, the stream is on your left), and you pass deep clear pools offering numerous summer bathing possibilities.
After **39min** the path divides. Either veer left to the river and cross on stepping stones or veer right and two minutes later (**41min**) scramble down water-smoothed rocks and cross by an 'Indiana Jones' narrow plank and log bridge. This is an excellent bathing spot. You are now on the river's right bank, but just one minute later (**43min**) cross over to the left bank once again by barely adequate stepping stones. You'll see an OPEN AREA WITH A RUIN AHEAD of you. Turn left and continue along the river.
At **46min** reach a junction with the GR11, marked with the usual red and white paint flashes. Follow

58

Talaixà: take the time for the five minute walk up to the church.

the GR to the left, along the same river as before. At **51min** there is another divide, but you continue to climb to the right, through box woods and past flat fields.

By **54min** you are down by the river again which you cross by stepping stones; less than three minutes later the ruined hermitage and chapel of **Sant Aniol** appear just above you, built in the 11th century in the Romanesque style on a 9th-century site. The old refuge behind is derelict. Climb up and perhaps picnic here (**1h**).

Go to the **Font** (spring) **de Sant Aniol** (straight ahead of you when you stand with your back to the entrance to the refuge).* Take the path to the right of the *font* but, behind the *font*, turn left and follow the footpath across a usually dried-up river bed and through woods of giant sweet chestnut trees. There is plenty of opportunity to get lost here on side paths, so keep checking for the red and white stripes of the GR11. You climb continuously and after 15 minutes pass through a swing-close GATE WITH GR MARKINGS (**1h15min**). At **1h20min** a vertiginous drop to your left gives spectacular views of

the river below and across heavily-wooded mountain wilderness to the summit of Bassegoda in the northeast (1373m/4505ft). The path swings westwards and passes a large BOULDER (**1h33min**) on which a painted sign indicates that Talaixà is straight ahead. At **1h38min** pass through another self-closing gate. At **1h47min** you reach the ruined hamlet of **La Quera** — just how did they get anything to this spot? — and look around for your onward marking. You'll see it at the back of the hamlet, leading on up the valley, between the wall of a house and a hedge.

After another 13 minutes of steady climbing and faithfully following GR waymarks, you arrive at **Talaixà** (**2h**), a ruined hilltop hamlet with a 17th-century church and views east and west over paradise.

You *leave* the GR here to descend sharply left from the path you arrived on, going back down the same valley — but on the opposite side. There are limited yellow path markings here — *no* red and white GR markers. Remember the warning about loose stones: it will become important on this twisty

*Before continuing on the GR11 to Talaixà, you could take a 30min (return) detour from the *font* to the signposted 'Salt del Brull' waterfall.

and gravelly descent. The way becomes clear after a few minutes. At **2h45min** you reach the river again. Don't cross it; instead, follow a footpath running along the right-hand side of the river. At **2h49min** you reach the ruins of **Hostal de Ca la Bruta** and the lovely **Pont d'en Valenti** foot-bridge. Cross and ascend to the track on which you parked (**2h51min**). Then either turn left to the most northerly CAR PARK (**3h**) or right towards Sadernes.

Walk 6: ALTA GARROTXA — SANTA BÀRBARA DE PRUNERES

See map opposite
Distance: 14km/8.7mi; 3h45min
Grade: moderate, with an ascent of about 350m/1150ft
Equipment: stout footwear with gripping soles as a minimum, because some descending sections are littered with loose stones. See notes on 'Walking', page 38.
How to get there and return:
🚗 (Car tour 2): Just east of Castellfollit de la Roca, take the road GIP5233 for Montagut and continue to the hamlet of Sadernes, where there is a car park on the left (in front of the church, below the restaurant).
Short walk: Walk only as far as **Coll de Jou** (spectacular views) and return the same way (1h15min).
*Note and **warning**: On rare occasions, after prolonged, heavy rain, the Sant Aniol river bed may be **impassable**.*

The word *'garrotxa'* indicates a rugged landscape, where walking is difficult. Surprisingly, Bassegoda, the highest point of this spectacular region of Alta Garrotxa is only 1373m/4505ft, but the narrow, steep-sided valleys are tremendously deep. This itinerary provides uplifting views all over this tortured region, including Puig de Bassegoda, and makes a tranquil alternative to the popular Sant Aniol walk (Walk 5).

Start the walk at the CAR PARK in front of the church at **Sadernes:** follow the track straight ahead towards 'SANT ANIOL', always keeping left. After **5min** turn left down a narrow path waymarked in blue and signposted to 'SANTA BARBARA' and 'OIX'.
The path crosses the bed of the **Sant Aniol River** (normally dry, but you may have to rock-hop or paddle). Look out for a large rock on the far bank with the word 'OIX' painted on it. The path you want is *on top* of the rock and climbs steeply through evergreen oak woods.
At **20min** ignore a path to the left and continue ahead. At **37min** the path reaches the **Coll de Jou** (confirmed by a wooden sign) where there is a little stone-built house. Skirt the house, cross the pasture, and turn right (westwards) to pass through the col. From here there are imposing views ahead of the cliffs along the Beget Valley in the northwest, as

well as of Santa Bàrbara de Pruneres, nestling close to the summit ridge of the **Serra de Santa Bàrbara**.
At **49min** turn right onto a track and follow it for just two minutes (**51min**) before turning right once more onto a narrow path marked by CAIRNS. Soon you will have a clear view of the strangely-shaped Bassegoda in the northeast — looking like a bun on which someone has carelessly added an extra blob of dough.
At **1h07min**, just before a ruined house, swing leftwards and make your way up the grassy terraces to the 10th-century **Santa Bàrbara de Pruneres** (**1h16min**). From the church follow the track which begins by heading northwards but soon curls back southwards. Once clear of the woods there are splendid views westwards over the little village of Oix. Soon after the track passes a large FARMHOUSE, at a junction, turn left (**1h24min**).
At **1h36min**, at another junction,

61

Above: in summer the Riera de Sant Aniol at Sadernes is dried up. If you reach this point in the river bed, you have gone too far north. Retrace your steps, looking for the rock with the word 'Oix' painted on it. At other times of the year the river flows nicely, as here (left) at the Pont d'en Valenti (Walk 5).

2h16min, just after a chain, come to a junction and continue straight ahead. At **2h27min** leave the track, on a path bearing off to the right, and clearly marked with red and white stripes.

The path skirts the little shrine known as the **Oratori de Plansalloses** (**2h29min**). In **2h44min** the path widens to a track and descends to the tarmac road at the 12th-century stone footbridge, the **Pont de Llierca** (**2h49min**) — a miracle of medieval engineering. There is a *font* on the north side of the bridge, reached by a marked path from the road.

From here follow the road to the left, to the **Pont de Plansarenes** (**3h24min**). After crossing the bridge, take the clear track, then footpath westwards, signposted 'SANTA BARBARA DE PRUNERES'. After crossing the river bed twice, at **3h37min** turn right up the path you descended at the start of the walk, back to your car at **Sadernes** (**3h45min**).

carry straight on towards a RED-TILED FARMHOUSE. At **1h39min** pass the house (**Palomeres**) and at **1h42min** reach yet another junction, with a choice of two parallel tracks to the left. You want the first (*lower*) of these tracks, which is the GR1 footpath and occasionally marked by red and white stripes.

At **1h50min**, just beyond an opening in the forest, the way becomes a narrow path once more. Pass a RUIN at **2h03min** and a minute later turn right (eastwards) onto a track. At

Walk 7: A CANIGOU CANTER

Distance: 10km/6mi; 3h15min
Grade: moderate, with some scrambling and an ascent of more than 600m/1970ft *from the Chalet des Cortalets*
Equipment: mountain walking equipment appropriate to the season (Canigou is 2784m/9130ft high) — see notes on 'walking', page 38.
How to get there and return:
🚗 Pre-arranged jeep taxis to/from the Chalet des Cortalets (04 68 05 64 61, 04 68 05 62 28 or 04 68 05 63 06 or contact the Vernet-les-Bains Tourist Office 04 68 05 55 35; www.ot-vernet-les-bains.fr).
Or 🚗 (Car tour 2): Some 2.5km/1.5mi east of Prades, on the N116 Perpignan-Prades road, take the D24B signposted 'Los Masos, Villerach', and when it turns to track, keep ahead. Aim to get as

close to the Chalet des Cortalets (04 68 96 36 19, http://cortalets.over-blog.com) as you can — depending on the state of the track and the ground clearance of your vehicle. It is normally possible to get at least as far as the Refuge de Prat Cabrera (about an hour up by car, leaving another hour on foot to the Cortalets) but, given 4WD-type clearance and a little luck, you may be able to drive all the way.
Short/Alternative walk: Leave your transport on the track near the **Refuge de Prat Cabrera** and climb some 350m/1150ft to the **Chalet des Cortalets**, with its hostel-type accommodation, refreshments and meals (open summer only). Allow up to 3h there and back. If arriving by jeep-taxi simply follow the Canigou ascent as far as you wish.

A classic walk featuring the summit ascent of Canigou, at 2784 metres (9130 feet), one of the highest mountains of the region and a much-loved landmark, quite clearly visible from many Costa Brava beaches. Unlike the peaks further west, this is a Mediterranean mountain, free from ski-lifts, resin-scented and saturated with light.

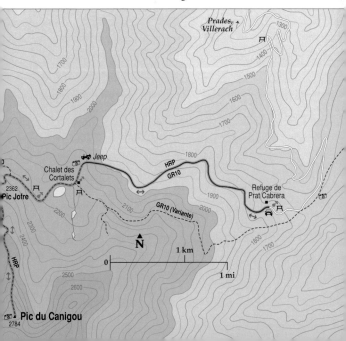

St-Martin-du-Canigou, near Walk 7 and Car tour 2

We start our timings from the **Chalet des Cortalets** (2150m/7050ft), a hideout for the Maquis during the Second World War. As you leave the chalet along the main vehicle track, a wooden sign for 'CANIGOU' directs you to the left. A clear footpath crosses a stream, skirts a LAKE (**15min**), leaving it to the left, and ascends westwards to the long ridge that leads to the summit.

After **25min** pass a PICNIC SITE with stone table and benches (drinking water nearby) and in **55min** come to the bottom of the final ridge. A clear path leads up the ridge, past large rock formations and views towards the rubble-strewn east face of the peak.

Reach the base of the summit cone in **1h10min**; from here a rocky path, sometimes difficult to discern, zigzags up to the top. *Take care;* it is steep and can be slippery. At this stage many walkers prefer to devise their own route up to the SUMMIT of **Canigou** (**1h45min**). After a minute or two to get used to the exposure and awesome views, take a look at the *table d'orientation*. Then descend by the same route to the **Chalet des Cortalets** in 1h30min (**3h15min**).

Descending from the summit in springtime can be exhilarating — or very dangerous, if you haven't the right equipment. Be sure to read the notes on high-level walking before you tackle any of the peaks.

Walk 8: CARANÇA CLIFFHANGER

Distance: 20km/12.5mi; 7h40min

Grade: moderate, but the climb of 1300m/4265ft for the full itinerary demands considerable stamina.

Equipment: good footwear is essential and a compass might prove useful on the return leg in poor visibility — see introductory notes on 'Walking', page 38.

How to get there and return:
🚂 (Petit Train Jaune) to Thuès-entre-Valls (the line runs from Villefranche-de-Conflent to Latour-de-Carol): for information telephone 04 68 96 56 62 or see www.trainstouristiques-ter.com; or 🚗 (Car tour 3): from Puigcerda take the N116 towards Perpignan and park in the car park below the railway station.

Short walks: Follow the main walk as far as the BALCONY (27min), but instead of turning left, turn right to return to the car park in a total of 1h; or, for a slightly longer version, continue

The 'Petit Train Jaune' is a familiar sight in the eastern Pyrenees between Villefranche and La Tour de Carol.

on the main itinerary until the FIRST OF THE LADDERS (53min), from where you can return to the car park along the river's right bank in a total of 1h40min.

Alternative walk: Once at the Refuge de la Carança you could simply return along your outward route, saving half an hour.

Useful contacts: Villefranche-de-Conflent Tourist Office 04 68 96 22 96, office http://france-for-visitors.com/pyrenees/roussillon/villefranche-de-conflent.html; taxis 04 68 05 64 61, 04 68 05 66 58

Few walks offer such dramas within so short a distance of the car park — a narrow gorge, spectacular rock formations and gravity-defying walkways. And that's just the start!

Begin the walk at **Thuès** by passing under the RAILWAY BRIDGE at the end of the car park (just downhill from the station). Immediately you are in the bottom of a narrow gorge, whose sheer, high walls are a promise of vertiginous thrills to come.

In **10min** you have a choice: you can turn right and cross the BRIDGE to follow our itinerary, but if you really have no head for heights, you can continue straight ahead to rejoin the main walk at the FIRST LADDER (the 53min-point). Beyond the bridge the path climbs to a BALCONY (**27min**). Turn left (south) to continue the walk (but by turning right you can make a

circuit back to the car park, with a total time of just under one hour). After thirty paces ignore the path that climbs up to the right (your return route). Your onward path has been cut into the rock face with the raging waters of the **Carança Gorge** now dizzyingly far below — take a good grip on the hand rail! The balcony runs more or less horizontally until, after 26 minutes (**53min**), you begin to negotiate a dazzling series of LADDERS AND BRIDGES. This continues for just over an hour, after which you emerge from the gorge (**1h55min**).

A clear path now remains close to the river, climbing easily as the

65

Spectacular rock formations in the Carança Gorge

valley gradually opens out. At **3h** take careful note of a CAIRN and a path that climbs back to your right (north); this is the return route. But for now carry on the extra 30 minutes to the **Refuge de la Carança (3h30min)**, where in summer refreshments await you. The refuge is a walkers' crossroads. The GR10 long distance footpath passes by, coming from the distinctive U-shaped col to the northwest (Coll Mitja) and crossing over the river in the direction of Mantet to the east. The celebrated Etang (Lake) de la Carança lies an hour and a half further south along the Carança River (if you have the energy). To return, retrace your steps to the CAIRN (**4h**) and take the path to the left. It climbs in hairpins away from the river and then traverses the slope to the **Las Tours** stream (**4h33min**). Cross the stream and continue past an *orri*. Some 15 minutes after the stream, leave a startling ROCK NEEDLE to your right (**4h48min**).

After another 17 minutes the path swings west to cross the **Roig** stream (**5h05min**), then climbs in hairpins amongst hazel and mountain pine before redescending to another stream.

Once across, leave another *orri* to your right.

At **5h55min**, where the path abruptly cuts back towards the southwest, the little **Dona Pa** refuge (unstaffed) is just off to the right. After 10 minutes (**6h05min**) the path swings round to the north once more — ignore the path to the left. Your path now zigzags down through oak woods (used in the construction of the 'little yellow railway') to rejoin your outward route (**7h20min**). Turn left.

After 30 paces you will see the path you ascended from the first bridge seven hours earlier dropping down to your right. But we are not yet finished with the spectacle. Continue ahead along a path with terrifying drops to the right (you're used to them by now) and beautiful views out to the Têt Valley. Once clear of the gorge, the path winds down to the car park in **Thuès (7h40min)**.

Walk 9: NURIA • GORGES DEL FRESER • QUERALBS

Distance: 16km/10mi; 6h20min
Grade: moderate. In the main, the walk is a descent of some 750m/2460ft from Núria.
Equipment: no special requirements — but see introductory notes on 'walking', page 38.
How to get there:  to Ribes de Freser and then onwards by *cremallera* — rack railway — to Núria. Or 🚗 (Car tour 2): from Ripoll head north to Ribes de Freser, park at the station (Ribes-Enllaç) and then take the *cremallera* to Núria. Departures from Ribes are at roughly hourly intervals throughout the day. The ascent takes 40 minutes. For all information on trains to Ribes, telephone RENFE 902 24 34 02

or see timetables online at www.renfe.com. For all information on the *cremallera*, telephone 972 73 20 20. The railway is closed in November each year.
To return: 🚂 *cremallera* from Queralbs back to Ribes de Freser. The last departure is around 22.00. For all information on the *cremallera*, telephone 972 73 20 20, www.valdenuria.cat
Alternative walk: Follow the walk in the opposite direction, heading downhill from Queralbs station to turn left over a BRIDGE in five minutes. Immediately beyond this bridge fork left up a concrete track which leads to HYDROELECTRIC BUILDINGS. Cross a second bridge to reach these buildings and then turn right to enter the **Gorges del Freser**. Penetrate as far as you wish. Easy to moderate, depending on how far you climb.
Note: This is a region savaged by

winter weather, and although the local authorities attempt to maintain safe river crossings, they do not always succeed. Bridges swept away by avalanches may be replaced by makeshift log crossings or by nothing. You must take special care here and bear in mind that finding suitable crossings may add substantially to walk times.

The adventure begins with a ride on the *cremallera* (rack railway; the last to function commercially in Catalonia) from the little stone-built mountain village of Queralbs. The steep track passes high cliffs, runs along the edge of deep chasms and penetrates rock-hewn tunnels, before depositing its load of passengers and goods at the terminus after some 15 minutes. This is Núria (1967m/6450ft), Catalonia's first international ski station and site of the Santuari de Núria, its traditionally ecclesiastical buildings now converted into a two-star hotel and refuge.

To start the walk at **Núria**, cross the RAILWAY LINE and take the red/white waymarked GR11.7 past the SKI LIFT, climbing above the line of the railway, which you keep to the right. You ascend past some unusual religious sculptures, after **10min** swinging left. In **20min** you'll see on your left a large concrete altar with a GIANT CROSS suspended above it. Stand on the track with your back to this and descend straight across pastureland (southeast, in the direction of the long part of the cross) — to a small footpath.

Follow this narrow earthen path over a shoulder and into a new vista — first bearing away towards the left to cross a stream and then southwards, cutting across the hillside towards a ridge. At **1h** reach a cairn and an OLD SIGNPOST, its lettering totally obliterated by time and weather. Here the path turns sharp left,

continuing more or less on the same contour, gradually joining a good path rising from a shepherd's ruined hut *(orri)*. Watch for the occasional bemused izard (Pyrenean chamois), curious at the sight of walkers slithering downhill.

Turn sharp left (east) at the *orri* and pick up a path, sometimes vague, that leads away from the Gorges de Núria and into the awesome **Gorges del Freser**. Cross the **Torrente de Coma de Gispet** at **1h25min**. The path now cuts a clear line across steep slopes, rising and falling, its surface alternating from loose stone to firmer rock. CAIRNS mark the way where necessary. For those with a hankering to yodel, this is a good spot, as the echoing calls of the chocards (choughs) demonstrate.

At **2h20min**, after a succession of often vertiginous views, you encounter the steepest descent of the walk. Follow the path close to the cliff. There may be cables to assist you on the more vertiginous stretches. At **2h35min** mount the last in a series of small rises and climb through a gap between rock 'teeth', the **Cingles de la Balma**, to arrive at a wide grassy COL

Fire salamander

giving views onto a new landscape. The path turns sharp left and climbs to a ridge, which you reach at about **2h50min**. The path is now clear and well-marked with cairns. At **3h** you mount a small rise to see the **Refugi Coma de Vaca** (1995m/6544ft) where, a few minutes later, you can be enjoying a cool drink and, if you wish, a meal.

From the area of the refuge, paths go off in all directions, but their exact positions can change from year to year because of snow damage. You now want to *leave* the GR11.7 and take the path through the bottom of the **Gorges del Freser** to Queralbs; this descends from the refuge to the **Riu Freser** and crosses by a small BRIDGE (at time of writing). A MARSHY SIDE-STREAM poses the next obstacle, normally crossed by walking up it until the ground is firm enough to pass.

Once across the side-stream descend westwards on a clear path with fabulous views of the sheer rock faces you negotiated all the way from the ruined *orri*. You reach the VALLEY FLOOR in **4h35min**. Cross the **Riu Freser** again via a precarious BRIDGE (or STEPPING STONES).

The walk now continues by following the clear path along the bottom of the valley, descending and crossing numerous streams. If it is evening, watch out for the nocturnal black and yellow fire salamanders, newt-like creatures so slow-moving that they run the risk of being trampled underfoot.

At **6h** reach a HYDROELECTRIC COMPLEX and turn left over a bridge in front of it, to walk the short section of concrete track to the tarmac Queralbs/Ribes road (**6h10min**). Turn right for the short climb to **Queralbs** STATION (**6h20min**).

The bald mountains above Núria

Walk 10: PEDRAFORCA

See also photos pages 8-9, 17
Distance: 9km/5.6mi; 4h
Grade: difficult, involving a strenuous ascent (sometimes over scree) of 1072m/3516ft over a distance of just 4.5km/2.8mi and descending the same way
Equipment: mountain walking equipment; you will ascend to 2498m/8193ft — see 'Walking' on page 38. Full water bottles (there is no water anywhere on the main itinerary); collapsible hiking poles are helpful; you might like to wear gloves for the descent over scree.
How to get there and return:
🚌 to Gósol (Car tour 3); park in the square in the centre (bar and restaurant). A limited bus service between Gosol and Berga is run by bus company Alsina Graells 902 42 22 42, www.alsa.es.
Short walk: go to the **Pla de la Serra** and back (1h25min; quite easy if taken slowly).
Alternative walk: Follow the GR107 (Camí dels Bons Homes) to the picnic spot at **Coll de Font Terrers** (also accessible by car — see Car tour 3) and from there to **El Collell** (1845m/6052ft), for its glorious views, returning the same way. Join the footpath by taking CARRER PICASSO from the square (Plaça Major), and then CARRER CERDANYA. The footpath, an easy climb of about 450m/1475ft, is well signposted and marked with both red/white and yellow/white flashes. Allow about 45mins to Coll de Font Terrers and 2h to El Collell (somewhat less for the return).
Useful contacts: Oficina del Parc Natural del Cadí-Moixeró 93 824 41 51 or www. gencat.net/ mediamb/parcs/cadi; Oficina d'Informació Paratge natural del Pedraforca 938 258 005; Gósol *ajuntament* (town hall) 973 37 00 55, www.gosol.ddl.net

Pedraforca (the name means forked rock) is one of the most famous mountains in Catalonia. Inside the beautiful Cadí-Moixeró Natural Park, the bizarre double summits, separated by a so-called *enforcadura* (fork) of scree, are a landmark challenging you to reach the summit. And, improbable as it may seem from the valley floor, you can! There are three main approaches. We are going to take you up the one that poses the least difficulty, which starts from Gósol. Do not let anybody convince you otherwise.

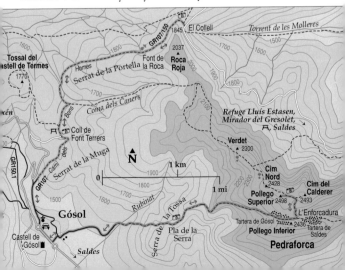

Set off from the fountain SQUARE at the centre of **Gósol** (where a plaque on a house commemorates a stay by Picasso). Amble along the CARRETERA GUARDIO in the direction of Saldes. Off to your left you will see the unmistakable Pedraforca and, in the foreground, TWO HOUSES a little separated from the village (they are shown in the photograph below). Just before the roundabout, take the track on the left and head towards those houses. The route is well marked by yellow and white flashes, all the way to the *enforcadura* — if you go very far without seeing these footpath signs, you have lost your way. At **5min** turn right, pass the houses and climb a gentle farm track. At **21min** the track runs out and you swing to the right to cross the stony bed of the **Rubinat** stream (normally dry). Now the path climbs steeply eastwards through the delightful pine woods on the flanks of the **Serra de la Tossa**, to emerge at a lovely clearing, the **Pla de la Serra** (**55min**). There are beautiful views from here over Gósol to the Serra del Cadí. *The Short walk turns back here.*

For the main walk, continue straight across the clearing, back into the woods, and along the spine. By **1h05min** the going gets even tougher, when the path emerges from the wood onto scree — the infamous **Tartera de Gósol**. If you have hiking poles, deploy them now. This loose stone is how it's going to be all the way to the *enforcadura*. But there is a clear path and, surprisingly, the going gets a little easier towards the top, where tufts of grass glue the scree down and provide footholds. Keep your spirits up-you're quite likely to see izards (the Pyrenean chamois).

At **2h** you reach the TOP OF THE **Enforcadura**. The main summit (Pollego Superior) is to your left (north), and if you've made it this

far, you can certainly make it all the way. From here on there are *no markings* at all, but you will see a faint path climbing up into the rocks where the boots of thousands of hikers have polished footholds and left clear traces. What looks from the valley like smooth rock is, in fact, a jumble of boulders which you can scramble up to reach the summit, **Pollego Superior** (**2h25min**), marked by a cross and a flag. Congratulations! You are standing at 2498m/ 8193ft and, with sheer drops all around, it feels like it!

On no account think of making a circuit by descending to the Collada de Verdet — it is an exposed and highly dangerous descent.

When you have finished taking in the awesome views, go back down to the *enforcadura* (**2h40min**). You're now going to have to retrace your steps over the scree, but console yourself

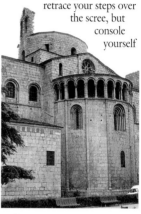

with the thought that the Tartera de Saldes, the opposite side of the *enforcadura*, is even worse. Initially seek out the grassy tufts, and lower down use the deeper scree to the side of the path. Turning your feet sideways across the path also helps. Inevitably you will slip down a few times — which is where gloves can be beneficial. At **3h15min** the scree is behind you, and 15 minutes later you can be relaxing back at the **Pla de la Serra** (**3h30min**) before your return to **Gósol** (**4h**).

Left and above left: Pedraforca from Gósol and the start of the walk (the itinerary passes close to the two houses in the photograph on the left). The 'collar' of scree, the enforcadura, *is clearly visible below the peaks. Top right: cathedral at La Seu d'Urgell, a good base for exploring the Cadí*

Walk 11: SANT-MIQUEL D'ENGOLASTERS • MADRIU VALLEY • REFUGI DEL RIU DELS ORRIS • SANT-MIQUEL D'ENGOLASTERS

Estany d'Engolasters

See also photograph page 1
Distance: 18km/11.2mi; 5h30min
Grade: moderate, involving only 550m/1800ft of ascent
Equipment: You'll be reaching over 2000m/6560ft; clothing must be appropriate to the conditions — see notes on 'Walking', page 38.
How to get there and return: 🚐 to Les Escaldes (376 82 04 12

or 376 80 70 00), then taxi (376 86 30 00, 376 32 31 11 or 376 32 37 43) to the lovely Romanesque church of Sant-Miquel d'Engolasters. Continue *past* the church towards the Estany (lake) d'Engolasters, and park at the final hairpin bend just before the lake (by a sign on the right, 'Circuit de les Fonts'). Pre-arrange a taxi for your return. Or 🚗: follow the description for taxis.
Stroll: Allow 1h30min for this easy 'figure-of-eight'. From the parking area continue uphill to the BAR-RESTAURANT and from there descend to the **Estany d'Engolasters**. Take the path below the dam and circle the lake, passing another bar/restaurant on the north side. Opposite the dam wall go left up the footpath with wooden railings, then return to the parking area. Now follow the main walk, taking time to climb up to the MIRADOR (with a plaque

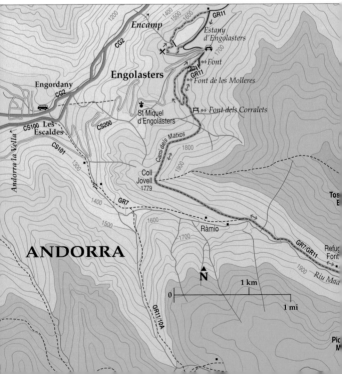

naming all the peaks around Andorra la Vella). Continue as far as the **Font dels Corralets**, then turn back. After three minutes turn sharp left down a path signposted 'CIRC. ESPORTIU'. This lovely grassy path rejoins the main track just short of the first *font*. Retrace your steps to the parking.

Short walk: Follow the itinerary just to **Fontverd** or just beyond **La Farga Vella**, and return the same way (2h30min-4h, depending on where you turn round).

Alternative walk: From the Refugi del Riu dels Orris, continue on the GR7 to the **Refugi de l'Illa** (2485m/8150ft) and the nearby lake, **Estany de l'Illa** (2510m/8233ft). Worth the extra effort, but allow an extra 1h30min up, and at least 3h to get back to your car/taxi (7h30min in total).

General information: Andorra la Vella Tourist Office 376 82 71 17, www.andorra.ad

---

Many of the larger Andorran valleys have been ruined by roads, building and ski development. This is one that, for now, remains beautifully unspoiled — a complete contrast to the hubbub of urban Andorra.

Start out from the 'CIRCUIT DE LES FONTS' SIGNPOST near the **Estany d'Engolasters** and follow the cinder track southwest uphill. It is marked with the red and white stripes of the GR11 and a sign indicating 'COLL JOVELL, VALL DEL MADRIU'. You pass a first *font* (spring) in **2min**. At **5min** the track narrows. Ignore the rough track coming in from the left, and go through a tiny TUNNEL. At the exit, a signpost indicates a MIRADOR off to the right. At **10min** the cinder track becomes a footpath (the CAMI DELS MATXOS), to ascend through the Molleres pine wood, and you pass the **Font de les Molleres** (**15min**). Seven minutes later, there is a large picnic area at the **Font dels Corralets** (**22min**), as well as

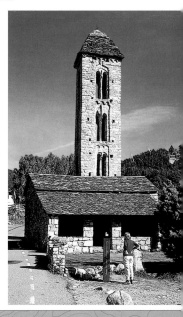

Sant-Miquel d'Engolasters

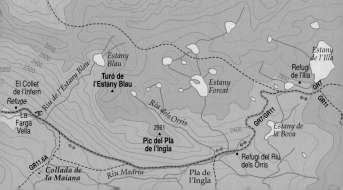

High in the valley of the Riu Madriu

another signpost indicating the ongoing route. *(The 'Stroll' turns back here.)* Soon you have a lovely view of Sant-Miquel d'Engolasters, as the path climbs more steeply to the **Coll Jovell** (1779m/5835ft; **30min**). Ignore the path to the left (to Tossa del Braibal) and continue on the GR11 which descends southeast into the idyllic Madriu Valley. At **45min** you join the GR7 footpath coming up from Les Escaldes, turning left (roughly eastwards) along the floor of the **Madriu Valley**, never far from the river.

Now simply amble along the valley, enjoying everything. At **Fontverd** (1873m/6143ft; **1h 25min**) there is a refuge and a *font*, and at the Collet de l'Infern (1970m/6462ft; **2h**) there is an old refuge. Just beyond lies **La Farga Vella** (**2h15min**), a flat, open area where iron was worked.

Keep going and you will come to a gorgeous area to just sit and commune with the scenery.

Soon the footpath divides. Ignore the GR11.6A, which hugs then crosses the river to Collada de la Maiana, instead continuing on the well-trodden GR7/GR11. The path continues to climb gently along the Madriu Valley, the river curving away to the right before joining the footpath once again at the large, flat pasture known as the **Pla de l'Ingla** (2180m/7150ft; **3h**). At the far end is the **Refugi del Riu dels Orris** (**3h15min**), a basic shelter sleeping just six people, and the end of our walk. Enjoy your picnic in this beautiful spot, with streams coming down from almost every direction, and the summit of Portelleta to the south.

Return by the same route to the 'CIRCUIT DE LES FONTS' SIGNPOST in around 2h15min (**5h30min**).

Walk 12: MOURGOUILLOU VALLEY • ETANG DE COMTE • ETANG DE COUART • ETANG VIDAL • ETANG DE COMTE • MOURGOUILLOU VALLEY

Distance: 12km/7.5mi; 5h30min from the car park (but 7h10min for hikers arriving by train)

Grade: moderate as far as the Etang de Comte, but thereafter suitable only for the fit and agile, with a climb of some 780m/ 2560ft and some scrambling over boulders — hard work!

Equipment: compass, map (such as Randonnées Pyrénéennes Cerdagne-Capcir), strong and waterproof footwear. Much of the walk is at 2000m: see introductory notes on 'Walking', page 38.

How to get there and return:
🚗 (Car tour 4): from Tarascon-sur-Ariège take the N20 south via Ax-les-Thermes and through Mérens-les-Vals; 700 metres beyond the village, where a dual carriageway begins, turn right to the campsite and then follow the forestry track that climbs up into the Mourgouillou Valley. Park in

the car park at the waterfall.

Or 🚂 to Mérens-les-Vals. The line runs from Toulouse to La Tour de Carol (for information telephone SNCF: 08 36 35 35 35/ freephone within France 08 05 90 36 35 or www.sncf.com). To reach the start of the walk from the station, head south along the main road, cross the Ariège River by a stone bridge (4min) and follow the red and white stripes of the GR10 along the Mourgouillou Valley, climbing to the parking place described above for motorists. (This adds 400m/1h of ascent; allow an extra 40min for the descent.)

Short walk: Turn round at the **Etang de Comte** (1h40min return) or at the **Jasse des Estagnols** (4h15min return).

For general information: Ax-les-Thermes Tourist Office 05 61 64 60 60, www.vallees-ax.com

Black Mérens horses, famous for their possible link with the wild horses of European prehistory, are often seen grazing along the Mourgouillou River valley, the setting for the first part of this walk.

From the CAR PARK by the WATER-FALL in the **Mourgouillou Valley**, take the forestry track that climbs east, quickly turning right onto a steep stone-slabbed path that is marked with the red and white stripes of the GR10. Where the forest opens out to a beautiful plateau, cross the river by the bridge known as the **Pont de Pierre** (15min). Beyond the bridge, turn left and continue up the valley by a succession of steep climbs and small plateaux, until you reach a tiny lake, only about 30m/100ft long (**L'Estagnol**; 45min). If you are lucky, you may see Mérens horses grazing here. Just beyond this lake, *leave* the

GR10 (which climbs steeply to the right) and continue along the valley to the first big lake, the **Etang de Comte** (1h). *This could be the ideal turn-around point for those taking the Short walk.*

The next section is physically demanding, though not too difficult technically. The ability to use a compass would be a great advantage — remember that the red and white GR10 flashes are no longer there to help you.

Pass around Lake Comte, keeping it to your right, and continue climbing along the valley, heading for the pass that you can see ahead. Keep the main stream a little away to your right, and aim also to clip the edge of the birch stand below the pass. (If you have a compass, the bearing is west-southwest.) Some 25 minutes after starting from the tip of the Etang de Comte, the path crosses a small side-stream WATERFALL (**1h25min**), where the water gushes out of a rock. Some 45 minutes beyond the lake, the path swings to the right of a mound and curves towards the main stream (**1h45min**). Climbing a little further you'll reach the **Jasse des Estagnols** and a small lake (usually dried up), from where you'll see a prominent rocky lump ahead in the middle of the valley — and sheer cliffs to the right, creating a defile that you will enter. After passing the dried-up lake to your right, cross to the

opposite bank beyond the lake, using a subtle line of STEPPING STONES. At **2h** cross a side stream and continue on the path which, in another ten minutes, disappears into a pile of rocks. This is just a foretaste of the chaos to come. The way is indicated by CAIRNS and always climbs along the valley, keeping the rocky lump to the left. The exact line may be tortuous, but there is no chance of getting lost, since the steep sides of the valley force you towards the **Etang de Couart**, which you should reach after **3h20min** of effort.

With luck you may see Egyptian vultures here in summer. Standing at the tip of the lake with your back to it (that is, facing east), a

Etang de Comte

valley opens up in front of you, with an obvious path down through it, and steep cliffs to the right. This is the return route. Head off along the path and come to the **Etang Vidal** (**3h45min**), passing along the narrow strip between its northern edge and a small but impressive rocky bluff. Continue in the same direction as before. The path is not always clear, but you have only to follow the valley as it descends gradually northeast. Finally, the path swings around northwards and drops rapidly, back to the **Jasse des Estagnols** (**4h15min**). From this level plateau, retrace your steps to the CAR PARK by the WATERFALL (**5h30min**).

Walk 13: GORGEOUS GORGES DE LA FRAU

See also photograph pages 18-19
Distance: 10km/6mi; 4h15min
Grade: easy; a gentle climb of 400m/1315ft at the end of the walk
Equipment: no special equipment necessary
How to get there and return: 🚗 (Car tour 4; park at the entrance to Comus). Transport is difficult for those who do not have a car; for information about buses and taxis telephone the *gîte d'etape* at Comus 04 68 20 33 69, www.gites-comus.com or the Ax-les-Thermes Tourist Office 05 61 64 60 60, www.vallees-ax.com.
Short walk: To save 6km/2h, drive down the white stone track at the southern entrance to Comus and continue some 3km to the obvious START OF THE GORGE (where the track swings up to the left); park here. Even better: companions willing, arrange to be dropped off at the begining of the gorge and picked up at the start of the tarmac (D5) at the other end (see map; 40min, very easy).

On the northern part of the Ariège-Pyrénées, like some 'lost world', the Plateau de Sault is forgotten France. To climb up from Ax-les-Thermes is to go back through centuries, when agriculture was not an industry and birds of prey were not hunted out of the skies. Today, cavers flock here, to the tunnels and gorges that penetrate the plateau. The most stunning of all are the Gorges de la Frau.

Choughs above the Gorges de la Frau and (below): landscape near Comus

At the southern entrance to the small village of **Comus** you'll see an *IRON CROSS* at the left of a crossroads of tarmac and motorable track. **Start walking** along the track leading straight on, below the village. The regular red and white waymarks of the GR7 route now appear. After a few minutes, pass a small *SEWAGE PLANT* (it passed our sensitive sniff-test as non-noxious). After **15min** come to some low grass-topped cliffs. The track is now descending through fir and beech trees. After **25min** fork right (the track rising on the left is marked clearly with a red and white cross — 'wrong way'). Continue to descend gently, with cliffs rising on each side of you, until the track swings around sharply to the left (**50min**). Now the track ascends and is marked with a clear red and white 'wrong way' cross. Your path lies over the edge of a slight crest to the right of the bend — in effect carrying straight on into the **Gorges de la Frau**. As you follow the narrow path through fairly dense undergrowth and fallen trees, you immediately feel you've reached real gorge country. After **1h10min** you'll see before you a *SPECTACULAR CLIFF*, striped orange and grey with the water streaks of centuries. The awesome scale of the surroundings lends lilliputian dimensions to mere spectators. Hear the electric calls of the jet black *chocards* (choughs), whose favourite home territory you now enter. If you are lucky enough to have the gorge to yourself, you'll discover a wilderness, nothing but trees and weird mountain shapes … and the echoed buzzing of millions of insects.

Finally the path joins a *TARMAC*

ROAD (**1h30min**). Follow this quiet and attractive route for as long as you wish, through the dense woodland and strangely-shaped mountains (the setting is shown on pages 18-19). After five minutes (**1h35min**) see, high up on the right, a gathering of *NEEDLE-SHARP ROCKS* surrounding a central pyramidal peak — a group looking like some sculpted monarch and courtiers.

We chose to walk down the tarmac, through this wilderness of mixed conifer and decidious woodland, for 25 minutes (**1h55min**), before turning round and starting the long climb back. Anywhere along this road (D5 from Fougax-et-Barrineuf) is ideal for arranging pick-ups, if one of your party agrees to play taxi. Or retrace your steps for a little over 2h, back to **Comus** (**4h15min**).

Walk 14: AMONG THE LAKES

Distance: 10km/6.2mi; 6h
Grade: moderate, with 850m/2800ft of ascent
Equipment: good quality high-mountain walking equipment — you will reach 2476m/8120ft. See notes on 'Walking', page 38.
How to get there and return:
🚗 From Vicdessos (Car tour 5) take the D8 signposted to Auzat, and continue for 17.7km/11mi to the southernmost end of the Etang (lake) de Soulcem. Beyond a picnic site (11.3km/7mi) the road deteriorates and climbs above the dam wall. Continue beyond the far end of the lake, and park just before the 'Aire d'accueil', where

you will see a footpath sign indicating 'Etangs de la Gardelle'.
Shorter walk: Walk only as far as the Gardelle lakes (**Etangs de la Gardelle**; 2h), returning the same way (3h20min); the ascent is the same as for the main walk.
Easy walk: From the parking, stroll along the path by the **Ruisseau de Soulcem** as far as you like, and return the same way. (The path is known as the '**Chemin des Orris**' for the large number of stone shepherds' huts.)
General information: Tarascon Tourist Office 05 61 05 94 94, www.montagnedetarasconetduvicdessos.fr

This is the Ariège at its most awesome. On a warm, sunny day the high-mountain scenery is uplifting, and the lakes, beginning with the Soulcem, can be an inviting shade of blue. But if the weather should deteriorate, be warned that these bare, wind-blasted slopes in the shadow of Montcalm and Estats (the most easterly three-thousanders in the Pyrenees) can become quite vicious.

Begin the walk at the PARKING AREA: cross the **Ruisseau de Soulcem** by the bridge, following the sign 'ETANGS DE LA GARDELLE'.

Beyond the bridge, ignore the clear path to the right; climb the slope in front of you. You will see the words 'LAC GARDELLE' painted

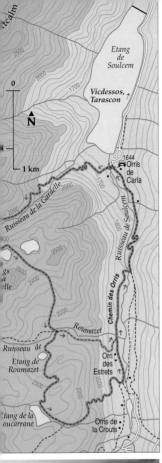

on a rock and the occasional YELLOW FLASH. A clear path gradually emerges, crossing the **Ruisseau de la Gardelle (30min)** and continuing along its left bank. In **1h30min** reach a pasture where only one of several *orries* (stone shepherds' huts) still stands intact. The path continues along the river to a marshy area, where it swings southeastwards to climb steeply to the first of the Gardelle lakes (**Etangs de la Gardelle**; 2370m/ 7774ft; **2h**). Take time to explore: a second, smaller lake lies to the southwest, and a third, much larger and extraordinarily round, beyond that. The crests to the west mark the Spanish frontier.

Return to the initial lake, following the marked path to a fourth lake lying to the east, from where the path climbs southeast into a COL marked by a large CAIRN (**2h30min**). Once through the col, the Etang de Roumazet is clearly visible below. The path descends to the **Ruisseau de Roumazet** (where it is met by another path leading down to the Soulcem plateau, should you wish to shorten the walk), then swings to the right to the **Etang de Roumazet** (2163m/7095ft; **3h15min**).

From the Roumazet lake, the path once again climbs in a southerly direction, and after 45 minutes we are at the final lake, the **Etang de la Soucarrane** (**4h**). From the end of this lake the path descends to the **Soulcem Valley**, initially along the outflow of the lake, and then bearing away to descend steeply into the valley bottom. Once on flattish ground again, you may still have energy left to enjoy the many *orries* that line the footpath (**Chemin des Orris**) back to the PARKING AREA (**6h**).

The Etang de Soulcem in deteriorating weather. On fine days, this lake makes an ideal picnic spot during Car tour 5.

Walk 15: CIRCUIT AROUND LAKE ARTAX (ARTATS)

Distance: 11.25km/7mi; 6h15min
Grade: moderate, with 1200m/ 3950ft of ascent
Equipment: normal mountain walking equipment; see 'Walking', page 38.
How to get there and return: ⊕ (Car tour 5). From Tarascon-sur-Ariège take the D23, signposted 'Parc Pyrénéen de l'Art Préhistorique'. Continue beyond the Parc to the village of Gourbit. In the village square follow the clear sign 'Etang d'Artax' and continue along an extremely narrow lane to a tiny parking area

1.2km/0.75mi from the village (room for about five cars).
Alternative walk: Cut out the Pic de Bassibié and the Pic de Boucarle, by heading straight from the lake to **Pla de Madame**, saving around 1h30min.
Short walk: Walk only as far as the **Etang d'Artax** (2h) and return the same way (3h20min).
General information: Tarascon Tourist Office 05 61 05 94 94, www.montagnedetarasconetduvic dessos.fr
Note: The name of the lake is variously spelt 'Artats' and 'Artax'.

T he Ariège, with its high mountains and deep valleys, has a reputation as the toughest region in the Pyrenees. This walk shows its gentler face, ideal when low cloud swirls around the frontier peaks.

Two paths lead away from the PARKING AREA south of **Gourbit**. One is signposted 'Col de Lastris' and is the way you will be returning at the end of the day. **Start the walk** by following the

route to the right, marked 'L'ETANG D'ARTAX', a truly delightful stone-slabbed footpath climbing southwestwards through beech woods. The path was renovated in 2002. Various other

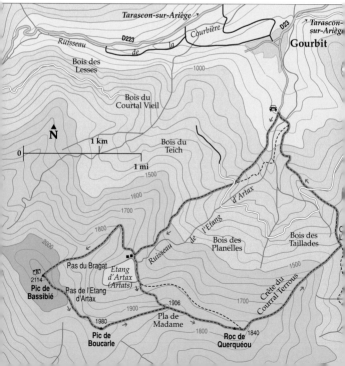

The delightful stone-laid path to Lake Artax

paths and tracks cross the route, but you will not go wrong as long as you follow the YELLOW PAINT flashes (and remembering not to enter paths marked with a yellow 'X').

In **2h** you reach the northeast corner of the **Etang d'Artax** (1695m/5560ft), where there are two little cabins. This is a kinder, softer Ariège than you'll experience on Walk 14, the lake nestling in the palm of grassy slopes. The big mound to the west is Pic de Bassibié, the next goal. *(But for the Alternative walk, strike out along the eastern shore of the lake and climb southeast directly to Pla de Madame.)*

To continue the main walk, take the little path that climbs northwards from behind the CABINS and, once on top of the ridge, simply head southwest to the **Pic de Bassibié** (2114m/6934ft; **3h30min**). From the top of this easy dome there are stupendous views west towards Mont Valier and east towards Carlit.

The itinerary now describes a semicircle along the southern crests that look down on the lake. Just stroll through the grass, past the **Pic de Boucarle** to **Pla de Madame** (*where the Alternative walk joins the ridge*; **4h15min**). Now continue to **Roc de Querquéou** (1840m/6035ft), where the ridge — the **Crête du Courral Terrous** — swings northeast and descends gently to the **Col de Lastris** (1427m/4680ft; **5h15min**).

At the col, a clear sign 'GOURBIT', indicates the way back to the PARKING AREA south of **Gourbit** (**6h15min**).

Walk 16: CRÊTE DES ISARDS

Distance: 11.5km/7.2mi; 7h
Grade: moderate, with about 850m/2790ft of ascent
Equipment: mountain walking equipment according to season (highest point 2381m/7810ft); see notes on 'Walking', page 38. The Riutort Valley can be quite boggy, so stout, water-resistant footwear is advisable.
How to get there and return:
🚗 (Car tour 5). From Tarascon-sur-Ariège take the N20 south to Les Cabannes. Turn into the village and follow signs for Aston and Barrage de Laparan (D520A). The road gradually deteriorates but is quite passable. Park after 20km, just beyond the dam wall, beside the little Riutort waterfall.

Shorter walk: From the **Cabane de Rieutort** go directly to the **Refuge du Rulhe** along the Riutort Valley, saving 1h30min. The path is well-marked (allow 3h to get to the Rulhe and 2h30min for the return by the same route).
Easy walk: From the parking area, amble beside the **Etang de Laparan** and as far along the valley as you wish.
Note: The Refuge du Rulhe (05 61 65 65 01, www.rulhe.com), the farthest point of the walk, is an excellent base for treks but is closed for redevelopment during all of 2011.
General information: Tarascon Tourist Office 05 61 05 94 94, www.montagnedetarasconetduvic dessos.fr.

The climax of this itinerary, the Crête des Isards, provides an exciting but safe ridge walk with marvellous views. Given the vertiginous drops on each side, you'll understand how it got its name.

Start out from the parking area at the **Riutort** WATERFALL, following the clear path signposted 'REFUGE DU RULHE' and marked with yellow flashes. The rocky path climbs very steeply at first, but after about **20min** of hard effort, you enter the pastures and follow the valley as it curves around towards the south.
At the **Cabane du Riutort** (**1h15min**; 1825m/5986ft), we leave the Riutort Valley footpath *(unless following the Alternative walk above)*. Do not cross the river by the bridge, but, instead, attack the slope to the east. This is not a marked path, but the open hillside, though steep, presents no problems. About half-way up, swing more to the north and in just under an hour reach the **Col de la Didorte** (2093m/6865ft; **2h10min**).
From here you will follow the

GR10, marked by red and white stripes, climbing southeast at first, and then swinging south as you make your way all along the ridge as far as the Col de Belh. The terrain is increasing spectacular, and onwards from the highest point (**Pic de Belh**, 2381m/ 7810ft) the ridge is very aptly

View along the Aston Valley from the Riutort Valley

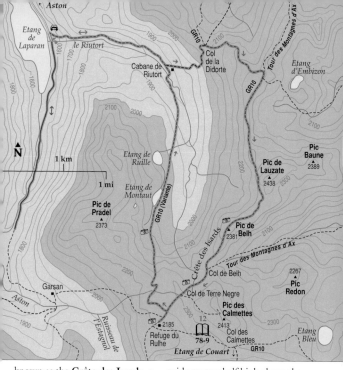

known as the **Crête des Isards**, a
reference to the agile Pyrenean
chamois. The ridge ends at the
Col de Belh (2247m/7370ft; **4h**).
Do not take the path northeast
here; instead take the path southwest to the **Col de Terre Negre**
and on down to the **Refuge du
Rulhe** (2185m/7167ft; **4h30min**),
a large, modern refuge built on a
wide grassy shelf high above the
Ruisseau de l'Estagnol.
After refreshments, take the path
clearly marked with red and white
stripes (a variation of the GR10)
along the **Riutort Valley** back to
the **Cabane du Riutort**
(**5h45min**), and then retrace your
steps to the **Riutort** WATERFALL
PARKING (**7h**).

Walk 17: PARC NACIONAL D'AIGUES TORTES

Distance: 10km/6mi; 3h50min *from the Estany de Sant Maurici*

Grade: moderate, with a climb of 350m/1150ft

Equipment: mountain walking equipment according to season — see introductory notes on 'Walking', page 38.

How to get there and return:
🚗 (Car tour 6, park at the Prats des Pierrós, at the entrance to the national park). Take a jeep-taxi to the lake and back. If you decide to walk — on a well-signposted footpath — allow an extra 250m/820ft of ascent (1h15min up, 45min back down).

Alternative walk: For the very fit! Continue to ascend from the Estanys de Monestero to the summit. Climb (with difficulty) a steeply zigzagging path to **Coll de Monestero** and then head to the right, keeping the top of the summit ridge to your right — terrific views. The final section to the **Pic de Peguera** (marked with cairns), is only recommended for very experienced mountain walkers. Add 750m/2460ft (3h20min) there and back from the Estanys de Monestero.

General information: Vielha Tourist Office 973 64 01 10, www.torismearan.org; Parc Nacional d'Aigües Tortes 973 69 61 89, www.gencat.cat and follow links to Parc Aiguestortes. Jeep/ taxis: Boi 973 69 63 14, Espot 973 62 41 05, www.taxiespot.com

Aigües tortes, literally translated, means 'twisted waters'. But the beautiful marshes, streams, waterfalls and lakes of the Parc Nacional d'Aigües Tortes have proved to be a curse. The waters are no longer free and rushing, but 'straightened out' — for hydroelectricity projects. One of only two national parks in the Spanish Pyrenees, the international status of Aigües Tortes with its 50 lakes is threatened. Our walk takes you to a part of the park that has almost escaped being tamed; for this pleasure we forego the luxury of way-markings in the later stages of the walk.

Alight from the jeep-taxi at **Estany** (lake) **de Sant Maurici**. The lake is beautiful when full, but bear in mind that the level can drop. **Start the walk** by heading south on the path that skirts the wall of the dam; it's signposted 'REFUGIO ERNEST MALLAFRE'. Soon the path divides; take the left-hand, lower route, which descends to a flat BRIDGE and passes the REFUGE (15min). The path (now signposted 'MONESTERO') zigzags steeply uphill, through flowers and thistles covered with butterflies, for which the park is well known. At **35min** start climbing through fir trees, keeping an attractive stream on the left. Boardwalks protect the marshy ground from erosion. Eventually a vast rocky lump materialises in front of you, and you keep it to your left, thus following the valley of **Monestero**, not Seca.

After **1h** find the 'lump' directly on your left and finish this easily-climbed section by arriving at a large plateau ringed by mountains — the **Prat de Monestero**. Now a stream lies left, and you pass little **Lake Feixant** and the larger **Estany Baix de Monestero** (**1h15min**). Beyond this lake the path is no longer as clearly marked, but there are some small CAIRNS. In **2h10min** climb steeply to another grassy pasture by the **Estanys de Monestero**. From here you can see straight ahead of you the Pic de Peguera (2982m/ 9780ft), the highest peak in this part of the park, slightly to the right of Monestero (2878m/ 9440ft), with the Coll de Monestero in between. The Estanys make a perfect picnic spot and base for the more demanding climb now facing those doing the Alternative walk to the summit. To return, retrace your steps to the **Estany de Sant Maurici** (**3h50min**).

Autumn in the Monestero Valley

Walk 18: A TASTE OF THE THE BARONNIES

Distance: 6km/3.7mi; 2h20min
Grade: easy climb of 250m/820ft; fairly steep descent at the end
Equipment: rubber boots advisable, otherwise no special equipment — but see introductory notes on 'Walking', page 38.
How to get there and return:
🚗 (Car tour 7 to Esparros). Esparros is easily accessible only by car, but there is an infrequent minibus service. For all information, plus details of accommodation, telephone the 'Maison des Baronnies' (summer only): 05 62 39 05 14 or try www.si-des-baronnies.fr, 05 62 40 93 01; or the Bagnères-de-Bigorre Tourist Office 05 62 95 50 71, www. bigorre.org. From Esparros village centre, drive downhill towards Laborde, and immediately after passing the *mairie* take the first left (south). After about 1.5km/1mi, you come to a crucifix and narrow track on your left signposted 'La Cascade': park here for the Short walk. For the main walk, continue along the road. At 4.5km/2.8mi from the village the tarmac ends at

a barrier, which is normally open. (If it should be closed, park as nearby as possible and continue on foot, adding 2.5km/1.5mi each way.) Beyond the barrier continue on good track and take the right fork just beyond the animal marshalling corral. You come to an exposed plateau at a crossroads of four tracks — the Col de Couradabat, where you should park.

Short walk (possible in dry weather only): Park by the huge CRUCIFIX (see above) and follow signs for 'LA CASCADE'. You'll pass through the flower-filled meadows shown below and reach an impressive moss-clothed WATERFALL (40min return). *The path can get very boggy and may be closed during wet spells.*

Alternative walk: To avoid the fairly steep descent from the grassy pass reached in 1h10min, return along your outgoing route (2h20min). But first climb the ridge, the **Crête de Sarramer**, and enjoy the view of the astonishingly remote country of these 'hidden' Baronnies valleys.

Below, opposite and overleaf: in the Baronnies

The Baronnies is an abandoned area, returning to nature — neither flat enough for modern agriculture, nor high enough for ski development. And what nature! We have seen *chevreuil* (roe deer), *sanglier* (wild boar) and *vautour fauves* (griffon vultures) in a single outing; the streams are believed to be home to one of the most elusive creatures of the Pyrenees, the *desman*, the aquatic mole-like animal with a trumpet-shaped nose shown here. We didn't see it — but you might.

Start the walk from the crossroads of tracks at the **Col de Couradabat**, where you should take the left-hand route (south) past a little stone *cabane* — often still used by shepherds and workers from the nearby mine. The track climbs up through beech wood. Go left at the only fork. As you near the top of the climb, you can hope to see vultures — we once did. That same day we also met up with an old *berger* (shepherd), who told us he had been camping out and watching his sheep for a week. He presented a marvellous example of travelling light — all he appeared to have in his tiny rucksack was a half-drunk bottle of wine!

The track makes for a low pass in the ridge. Ignore the divide which curves to the right and continue climbing ahead into the PASS (**1h10min**), pausing at the top, to look behind you for one of the most spectacular views you'll ever have of the more remote corners in the Pyrenees. *'Sauvage'*, say the French, to describe such a wilderness.

Be sure to visit the ancient abbey of Escaladieu on your way to Esparros (Car tour 7)

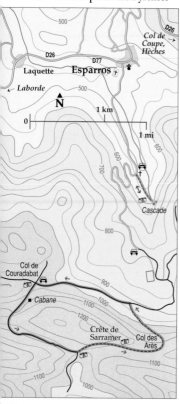

Ignoring the forestry track which continues ahead, pick up your ongoing footpath on the far side of the pass by bearing left (north). The path soon heads eastwards once more. It gradually rises up through box and pine (quite a few of the huge old pines are wreathed in lichen) to reach the top of a ridge, the **Crête de Sarramer** (**1h20min**). From here there are splendid views north to Esparros, and agricultural plains fill in the backdrop as far as the eye can see. Continue eastwards along the ridge, keeping a plantation fence to your left. At the **Col des Arès** (**1h30min**), abandon the ridge and take a left turn between this plantation and another. Your path descends steeply between the plantations and then into a dense forest of beech. At **1h40min** emerge from the beech into another fir plantation. Running through here, the path narrows, before joining up with the main track from Esparros at **1h55min**. Turn left to ascend back to the crossroads at the **Col de Couradabat** (**2h20min**).

Walk 19: THE ROOF OF THE PYRENEES

Distance: 7km/4.5mi; 5h
Grade: moderate — 1059m/
3475ft of quite demanding ascent
Equipment: mountain walking
equipment according to season —
see introductory notes on
'Walking', page 38. The final col
(Port de Venasque) is at a height
of 2444m/8018ft and is likely to
be in snow from November till
late spring.
How to get there and return:
🚌 (Car tour 7 to Luchon, from
where you continue south on the
D126 for 5km and then take the
left turn to the Hospice de France,
where there is a large car park).
Shorter walk: Go only as far as
the **Refuge de Venasque** for a
drink and a meal, then return the

same way: an ascent of about
850m/2800ft; 4h15min return.
The refuge, which has 30 places, is
staffed only from May to October
(check by telephoning 05 61 79
26 46 or 05 61 98 82 47).
Alternative walk: From the Port
de Venasque, the seriously fit can
easily ascend to the summit of **Pic
de Sauvegarde** (2738m/8980ft —
the mountain to the west of the
pass) by the clear path which
heads off to the right, from just
below the pass on the Spanish side
of the border. Allow 2h for the
round trip from the pass (making
7h in total).
For general information:
telephone the Luchon Tourist
Office 05 61 79 21 21.

Aneto (3404m/11,165ft), in Spain, is the highest peak in
the Pyrenees. An ascent is outside the scope of this book,
but the classic approach from the Hospice de France, near
Luchon, to the Port de Venasque, on the Franco-Spanish
frontier, makes a memorable day out in the historic footsteps
of many of the great 'Pyreneists'.

Looking back towards the Hospice de France from the top of the escarpment (just under 2h into the walk)

Start out at the CAR PARK by the **Hospice de France**, built by the Knights of St John of Jerusalem. Turn right, following the sign *'PORT DE VENASQUE'*. Cross the stream and follow the clear path through pasture and woodland, heading into a narrow valley and climbing a little west of south. After **14min** cross the stream on a concrete and metal BRIDGE. The path begins to climb more steeply in zigzags, and the valley closes in, allowing no possibility of getting lost.

After **1h** you arrive at the foot of a huge escarpment. Cross the stream on STEPPING STONES below the waterfall and continue up the grassy slope to the left of the rock face. At **1h25min** cross two small streams. After **1h45min** the path sweeps across to the centre of the valley, taking you above the escarpment. As you zigzag up, the views back are increasingly awesome. The Hospice de France is now only a dot in a green clearing, with the slopes of the Montagut range behind it, rising

94

up through forest to bare summits.

At **2h03min** you reach a crest and enter the upper valley. Your thighs can relax a bit. The refuge just beyond the crest is a ruin, but the Refuge de Venasque, where you are heading, is now only an easy 25 minutes away. Take the right-hand fork at **2h12min**.

When you finally reach the **Refuge de Venasque (2h30min)**, you will no doubt agree that its lakeside setting, beside the beautiful **Boums du Port**, is postcard-perfect. Two other, smaller lakes lie close by. *The Shorter walk returns from here.*

For the main walk, continue along the path to the east (without crossing the stream). After passing around a small rise, resume your southerly trajectory: the lake will be on your right and cliffs to your left. The path steepens on the northwest face of the **Pic de la Mine**, then enters a scree-strewn gully wedged between that mountain and the Pic de Sauvegarde to your right.

After 30 minutes of climbing from the refuge, a narrow pass suddenly opens in front of you. One more step through the **Port de Venasque (2444m/8016ft; 3h)** and you are in Spain. Savour the moment. Steeply below your feet lies the upper Esera Valley and beyond it the powerful Maladeta Massif, crowned by the Pico de Aneto.

Aneto was not conquered until 1842 (by a team led by the Russian climber, Platon de Tchihatcheff). The early explorers headed down into the Esera Valley before beginning the assault on the roof of the Pyrenees. You, however, will be returning by the same route to the **Hospice de France (5h)**.

Walk 20: CIRQUE DE GAVARNIE

Distance: 10km/6mi; 3h

Grade: an easy climb of 400m/1315ft — but the second part of the walk is dangerous if there is snow, in which case you should simply retrace your steps from the *cirque*, rather than continue.

Equipment: no special equipment, but see introductory notes on 'Walking', page 38.

How to get there and return: 🚐 occasional SNCF scheduled buses from Luz St Saveur 08 36 35 35 35/freephone within France 08 05 90 36 35; or 🚗 to Gavarnie (Car tour 8; obligatory parking in the car park at the entrance to the village). For further information, telephone the Gavarnie Tourist Office 05 62 92 49 10, www.gavarnie.com

Short walk: After reaching the **Hotel du Cirque**, return to Gavarnie by the same route (2h10min; easy).

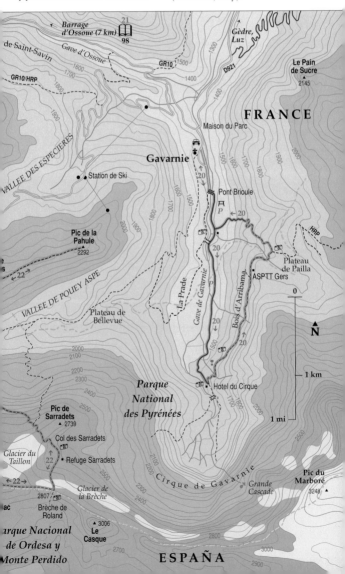

Gavarnie is a very popular climbing and walking centre in the Pyrenees and its *cirque* is one of the great spectacles of the world. If you're in the area on no account miss this — but, since it attracts more than half a million visitors a year, *do* avoid weekends. The glacier-scoured wall of rock, rising more than 1300m/4265ft from the valley floor and with a circumference of over 3km/2mi, is visible from some distance. As you approach the village, watch out, too, for the famous Brèche de Roland (photograph pages 100-101), the gap in the top of this rock wall. According to legend, the *brèche* was smashed out of the rock by the dying Roland, commander of Charlemagne's rearguard (see Walks 28 and 29).

Starting out from the centre of **Gavarnie**, take the same route as the *muletiers,* and head south towards the *cirque.* (If you prefer, you can take the pony-ride.) After **5min** cross the **Pont Brioule** by the Bergerie Café, where the tarmac road becomes track, and continue along the 'rive droite'. After **10min**, just before a modern barn, pass a path to the left, signposted 'Espuguettes' — this is the way you will be returning later in the day. For now, continue beside the river, the **Gave de Gavarnie**, which has its source high up in the glaciers of the *cirque.*

The track soon rises steeply until, after **20min**, you top the crest of a hill for your first view of the beautiful **La Prade** plateau. You are now within the Parc National des Pyrénées which links up, at the

top of the *cirque*, with the Ordesa National Park in Spain (see Walk 26).

Beyond the plateau the track rises up through the trees to a narrow gorge, at the end of which the **Hotel du Cirque** (**1h05min**) sits just out of reach of the midday shadow. Once the hotel hosted the 'greats' — from Russell (see Walk 21) and Charles Packe, to Gavarnie's last high-mountain guide, George Adagas. Nowadays, sadly, it is open only for refreshments and souvenirs. This is as far as the ponies go but, if you wish, you may continue to the foot of the **Cirque de Gavarnie** itself and cool off in the spray of the Grande Cascade (allow 1h30min extra). The return to Gavarnie may be by the same route (Short walk), but a more interesting alternative is to take the path that climbs up through the Bois d'Arribama, a wood offering welcome shade on a

hot day. From in front of the Hotel du Cirque follow the sign *'GAVARNIE PAR LES ESPUGUES'* and ascend northwards on a narrow path that passes along the side of the hotel. In five minutes (**1h10min**) you mount a small crest, from where there are good views back to Gavarnie. After another five minutes the path passes under high cliffs and at one point over an avalanche slope. (If there is snow, this section is *dangerous,* so take local advice before setting off on this part of the walk.)

After **2h** the path divides; take the upper right-hand path, in two minutes reaching a HUT belonging to 'ASPTT Gers'. From here there are views of the twin peaks, Petit and Grand Astazou, and the Couloir Swan separating them (southeast), Pailla Rouge (the 'red rock', east), and Pimené directly ahead (northeast).

After some **2h10min** cross a bridge to emerge onto the **Plateau de Pailla**, a superb vantage point and picnic area. From the plateau the path descends northwest and then zigzags towards Gavarnie, rejoining the original path at the barn ten minutes from the Bergerie Café. Turn right to the centre of **Gavarnie** (**3h**).

Cirque de Gavarnie from the Granges de Saugé (on the GR10 route, north of Gavarnie)

Walk 21: RUSSELL'S CAVES

See also photograph on pages 26-27

Distance: 12km/7.5mi; 4h30min

Grade: moderate — involves a strenuous ascent of some 750m/2460ft (up to 2500m/8200ft), and the crossing of permanent snow

Equipment: Study the introductory notes on high-mountain walking (page 38): in early or late season crampons, ice-axe and gaiters may be required. Water is plentiful.

How to get there and return:
🚕 taxi to the Barrage (dam) d'Ossoue from Gavarnie (from the Café Glaciers, telephone 05 62 92 47 30); or 🚗 to the Barrage (dam) d'Ossoue (Car tour 8: take the road out of Gavarnie towards the ski station and, at the first hairpin bend, follow the 'Ossoue' sign). The first 4km are on tarmac, the remaining 3km on track; pre-arrange with the taxi driver for your return. Or on foot from Gavarnie to the dam (only for the *ultra*-fit)!

Short walk: Follow the main walk to the top of the FIRST CASCADE, then retrace your steps (2h return; easy climb of 200m/650ft).

Alternative walk: Fit walkers may wish to continue along the path from Russell's caves for a further three-quarters of an hour to the **Refuge de Baysselance** (staffed from June 20 to September 20; 05 62 92 40 25, www.refuge.baysselance.free.fr). Another possibility is to get closer to the **Glacier d'Ossoue** by taking the cairned path on the left, beginning about 200m past the caves and climbing along the base of **Petit Vignemale**. *It is not advisable to walk on the glacier without rope and crampons and the knowledge of how to use them.*

Useful contact: Gavarnie Tourist Office 05 62 92 49 10, www.gavarnie.com

Count Henry Patrick Marie Russell-Killough (1834-1909) was one of the great traveller-eccentrics. His early explorations took him all over the world, but such became his obsession with the Pyrenees, and especially Vignemale (3298m/10,820ft), that he had a series of caves cut into the mountain where he lived and entertained for part of the year. The most accessible are the Grottes Bellevue, near the largest glacier in the Pyrenees.

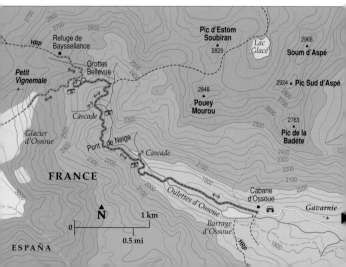

Looking south across the Barrage d'Ossoue

Starting from the end of the track along the **Ossoue Valley**, take the path that keeps the **Barrage d'Ossoue** to the left. Beyond the lake the path continues to a concrete bridge over the **Oulettes d'Ossoue** (**35min**) and then zigzags up to the top of a FIRST CASCADE (**1h**), after which it descends towards the stream (and an attractive picnic spot). *The Short walk turns back here.*

After **1h30min** you will reach the place known as the '**Pont de Neige**' (snow bridge) where, in the past, there was always permanent *névé* (porous ice formed from old snow). When we wrote the first edition of this book it was always at least 30 paces across but, due to climate warming, it may be reduced to no more than a few paces in August. However, always exercise great care here, especially in spring and autumn, when the snow may be extensive.

After **1h55min** the path tops a rise, and you'll see to your left the CASCADE that is fed by the Ossoue Glacier, the largest glacier remaining in the Pyrenees. Behind you there is a magnificent view of the frontier peaks and the Brèche de Roland (Walk 22). Crossing the stream below the cascade (on stones) you may wish to collect water.

From the stream climb in steep zigzags until you come to a wall of rock protruding from the scree. Cut into it are **Russell's Caves** — the **Grottes Bellevue** (**2h50min**). And what a view! — to the west the foot of the Ossoue Glacier, to the south the massif of Monte Perdido, the Brèche de Roland and Taillon. Russell's own cave, with a stone sleeping platform, is high enough to stand up in. Stay a while to contemplate the passion of this extraordinary man and the scene, a century ago, when he entertained society friends on his 'estate'.

Returning by the same route, you will be back at the **Barrage d'Ossoue** in just under 2h (**4h30min**).

Walk 22: BRECHE DE ROLAND

Distance: 12km/7.5mi; 6h
Grade: difficult — involves a climb of some 500m/1640ft and crossing the Glacier de la Brèche; but you will have lots of company! The description below is of summer conditions; the rest of the year this route is suitable only for mountaineers and ski-mountaineers with proper equipment and skills.
Equipment: mountain walking equipment appropriate to the season — see introductory notes on 'Walking', page 38.
How to get there and return:
taxi from Gavarnie (Café Glaciers, telephone 05 62 92 47 30). Pre-arrange a taxi for the return. Or (Car tour 8): drive to Gavarnie and then take the road to the ski station, parking at the Col de Tentes.
Short walks: Go as far as the **Refuge des Sarradets** for a magnificent view of the *brèche*, then retrace your steps (4h; easy climb of 300m/985ft). Or, from the parking at the Col de Tentes,

take the path eastwards that leads first to **Pic de Tentes** (2322m/7616ft) and then the **Pic de la Pahule** (2292m/7518ft), for some of the most impressive panoramas you will ever witness. An easy 2h there and back.
Alternative walk: The ultra-fit can continue through the *brèche* to the summit of the **Pic du Taillon** (3144m/10,312ft) and thus 'bag' an easy three-thousander. Once through the *brèche*, take the clear path to the right (westwards), first of all under the walls of the **Pic Bazillac**, past the 'finger' of the so-called *fausse* (false) *brèche*, and then along the ridge. The ascent poses no problems, but will add 2h 30min to your times — the views are well worth it if you have the energy.
Useful contacts: Gavarnie Tourist Office 05 62 92 49 10, www.gavarnie.com; Refuge Sarradets/Refuge de la Brèche de Roland 05 62 92 40 41 or 06 83 38 13 24, www.pyrenees - refuges.com(staffed 1/5-1/10).

A classic walk of the Central Pyrenees, this hike takes you to a gap in the wall of rock that forms a natural frontier between France and Spain. Legend insists that this curious breach in solid rock was caused by a blow from Durandel, the indestructable sword thrown by Roland when he was mortally wounded by his Saracen foe at Roncesvalles (see Walk 29).

Our timings start from the CAR PARK at the **Col de Tentes**. Follow the remains of an ice-fissured tarmac road southwestwards for 2km/1.25mi, high above the **Pouey Aspé Valley**, to the frontier pass known to some as the **Port de Gavarnie**, and to others as the **Col de Boucharo (30min)**. Do not go through the pass. Instead, take the steep path heading back eastwards along the opposite rim of the Pouey Aspé.

Brèche de Roland

Pass a 'PARC NATIONAL' sign warning you of the dangers of high-altitude mountain walking. And indeed, this is an area fraught with avalanches, stone-falls and, because of the high altitude, sudden weather changes. But the path is clear, and *on a fine day this is an expedition well within the reach of most fit walkers*. The sharp ascent ends after about **36min** at a huge BOULDER-STREWN PLATEAU under the north face of **Taillon**, a mountain much loved by climbers. The **Glacier des Gabiétous** is visible to the right.

After **1h30min** draw level with the far end of Taillon, where the path begins to rise sharply to the right. At **1h50min** come to a large rock with painted waymarkings on it — an arrow pointing down to Gavarnie by the route you would have travelled had you walked up from the village. Red marks also show the route to the *refuge* and *brèche,* but are surplus to requirements, as the path is clear, ascending a wide gully, sometimes running with water and with CHAINS to help you on the more difficult sections.

After **2h** you see ahead the strange MONOLITHIC ROCK known as the *'fausse* (false) *brèche'.* Closer to the path are some strangely striated cliffs, giving a foretaste of the landscape in the canyons of the Spanish Ordesa (Walk 26). Climb for five minutes more (**2h05min**) and pass the **Glacier du Taillon**, quite close on your right.

At **2h25min** reach the **Col des Sarradets**, for your first view of the refuge and your first close-up of the amazing Brèche de Roland. You reach the stone-built **Refuge des Sarradets** after **2h40min**. Have a rest, buy some refreshments (or indeed stay the night — the refuge is open all summer) and enjoy the most stupendous views of the Cirque de Gavarnie.

Then follow a faint path climbing the spine of a vast SCREE-SLOPE, to reach a plateau below the *brèche* (**3h10min**). You are at the foot of what little is left of the centuries-old **Glacier de la Brèche**, a mass of ice often covered with snow, invariably slippery and difficult to negotiate. However you'll be in the company of many other people, of all ages and abilities, some leaping up with the help of crampons and ice axes, others picking their way gingerly over patches of less slippery snow.

The **Brèche de Roland** (**3h 30min**) opens up one of the world's great views. In clear weather you can see rank after rank of the differently-coloured rock walls of Spain's famous canyons. Sunset here is magical. Step through and you're in Spain.

Return by the same route to the **Col de Tentes** (**6h**).

Sharing the trail with some mules, just before the Refuge Wallon (Walk 23)

Walk 23: PONT D'ESPAGNE • VALLEE DU MARCADAU • REFUGE WALLON • LAC DU POURTET • PONT D'ESPAGNE

Distance: 23km/14mi; 6h45min
Grade: moderate, with a climb of 950m/3115ft
Equipment: stout shoes; see also notes on 'Walking', page 38.
How to get there and return: taxi from Cauterets to Pont d'Espagne (05 62 92 53 68 or 05 62 92 61 62); or 🚗 (Car tour 8) park at Pont d'Espagne. Pre-arrange a taxi for the return.
Short walk: Go as far as you like along the Vallée du Marcadau and return by the same route — to the **Refuge Wallon** and back will take about 3h30min (an easy climb of some 300m/985ft).
Alternative walk: From Pont d'Espagne the GR10 footpath ascends the right bank of the river to the **Lac de Gaube**. This is an

easy, lovely, popular walk (just over 200m/650ft of ascent; 2h return). Refreshments are available at l'Hôtellerie du Lac de Gaube (06 37 44 38 64, www.gaube-seyres.fr). Return the same way or take the track to the top of the chair life (just 20min from the lake) and ride down.
Note: The Refuge Wallon is sometimes closed, even in peak season. If you plan to eat there, telephone before setting out. The same is true for the Hôtellerie du Lac de Gaube. Always carry refreshments with you!
Useful contacts: Cauterets Tourist Office 05 62 92 50 50, www.cauterets.com; Refuge Wallon (staffed mid-June to end-September) 05 62 92 64 28, www.pyrenees-refuges.com

The Marcadau is one of those rare Pyrenean valleys that has something of the ambiance of the 'Grand Nord'. It leads to the Refuge Wallon, with its feeling of high-mountain isolation, and from there the route climbs steeply to the lakes of Nère and Pourtet, before descending again towards Pont d'Espagne.

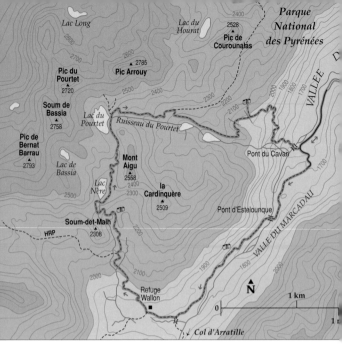

Start out at **Pont d'Espagne** (1460m/4789ft) and take the road to the **Chalet Refuge du Clot**. Cross two bridges over the **Gave du Marcadau** and turn right onto a tarmac road (closed to traffic), following signs to 'MARCADAU'. The road takes you westwards through a forest of silver fir until, after **45min**, you round a corner to see the open floor of the **Vallée du Marcadau** surrounded by high peaks, the stream sparkling in the sunshine. The road now becomes a jeep track and makes for the head of the valley, keeping the stream to the right.

After **1h** reach a collection of signs and turn left for 'VALLÉE DU MARCADAU/REFUGE WALLON'. The jeep track ascends through woodland, at **1h25min** emerging into an open area in the upper valley, where there are pleasant picnic spots beside the stream. Cross the stream on the **Pont d'Estalounque** and then continue along the opposite bank, after ten minutes climbing steeply through firs and then Scots pine. A small

PLATEAU (**1h50min**) gives you some magnificent views along the river, which is now far below. After **2h05min** come to 'PARC NATIONAL' signs. Ignore the left turn over the bridge (towards the Col d'Arratille) and continue on, to reach the **Refuge Wallon** in five minutes more (**2h10min**). Standing at 1866m/6120ft, this is one of the more substantial refuges, with refreshment, meals, and accommodation (closes around 25th September, only the petit refuge for mountaineers then remaining open). *The Short walk turns back here.*

To continue on the main itinerary, follow the sign 'LAC NERE, LAC DU POURTET'. Cairns mark the clear path which climbs northwest, cutting between ancient pines, their massive roots ready to trip up the unwary. Follow the path to the right and, at **2h25min**, you begin to zigzag steeply up through a maze of water- and animal-eroded paths. The official path is marked with the occasional CAIRN, but any route to the top will do.

After slightly less than ten minutes (about **2h35min**) use STEPPING STONES to cross a vigorous stream (don't miss an opportunity to fill water bottles here) and follow the path for another 20 minutes, when another obvious stepping-stone stream crossing will present itself on the left (**2h55min**). Do *not*, however, be tempted to take this, as you should keep the stream on your *left*. Look ahead and see your path zigzagging up the hillside. Come to a GRASSY PLATEAU and note a tall GREEN- AND YELLOW-PAINTED POLE which, like the stream, you keep to your left. Start to climb quite steeply again and at this point look behind for fantastic views of Vignemale (see Walk 21). The path levels out at **3h**, but after a short while the hard work starts again for another 10-minute climb to another GRASSY PLATEAU (**3h10min**).

Still keeping the stream on the left, walk across this plateau towards the mountains ahead. You're wondering how any path can manage to scale such steep cliffs. Worry not: as is often the way with footpaths, this one picks a perfectly manageable route, and the well-cairned path zigzags up, to deposit surprised walkers at the edge of the idyllic rock-ringed mountaintop **Lac Nère** (**3h45min**).

The path rises quite quickly from the right-hand side of the lake, continuing northwards, leaving the bowl at its far end. Note the occasional red waymarking and cairns — though the path is quite clear. After some 10 minutes' climbing (**3h55min**), come to a moonscape of loose rocks ringed by mountains. In the company of your own echo, pick your way straight ahead over rocks, following cairns and splodges of red paint, to climb to a second lake — the **Lac du Pourtet** (**4h15min**).

Follow the path along the right-hand side of the lake, until it turns right (east). Do not be tempted to walk to the tip of the lake. Your path comes to a ridge and then starts its long, long descent — rather steeply at first — over slippery rubble, to the first of several LOWER LAKES (**4h30min**). The tree-covered slopes of the Vallée du Marcadeau, your goal, come into view. Watch out for fleet-footed izard (Pyrenean chamois) here.

At **4h50min** come over another rise and take the lower of two paths offered, running beside the **Ruisseau du Pourtet**. At **5h** come to and pass another TWO LAKES in quick succession, after about eight minutes curving north to enter a new valley.

At **5h20min** the path begins to zigzag, crossing a stream and a boulder-strewn area. At **5h35min** it recrosses the stream and almost immediately divides. Take the right-hand fork (to the left there is a viewpoint), descending through increasingly dense woodland until, you reach the bottom, regaining your original route by crossing the **Pont du Cayan** (**5h35min**). Turn left and retrace the first section of the walk back to **Pont d'Espagne** (**6h45min**).

Walk 24: VALLE DE PINETA • COLLADO DE AÑISCLO • VALLE DE PINETA

Distance: 11km/7mi; 7h30min
Grade: very strenuous ascent of 1200m/3940ft, but not technically difficult

Equipment: proper mountain walking equipment, appropriate to the season — see introductory notes on 'Walking', page 38.

How to get there and return: 🚗 car (Car tour 9): park by the Refugio de Pineta for the standard walk, or (especially when there is a lot of water in the river) near the Camping Municipal for a longer itinerary which crosses the river by the bridge (Alternative walk). Or take a taxi from Bielsa (10km/6mi; 626 60 80 66 or 619 71 79 93), asking to be dropped either on the road near the *refugio* or at the Camping Municipal. Return by 🚗 pre-arranged taxi or your car.

Short walk: Turn back any time you like — the views are spectacular all the way.

Alternative walk: Begin and end the walk at the *parador*, which will add about 1h return.

Important: The full walk involves ascending to 2460m/8070ft, which means that there will be snow on the upper section between late October and late June. Do not flirt with steep snow slopes without proper equipment and experience; be content to turn around at the snow line and make a safe descent.

Useful contact: Bielsa Tourist Office 974 50 10 00, www.bielsa.com

*Left: Izard; below: Pineta Valley
Far right: Tres Marías waterfall*

From the road beside the Río Cinca, you'd think that only an izard (Pyrenean chamois) could climb the almost-sheer cliffs of the Sierra de las Sucas on the opposite side of the valley. But it would be a pity to leave such stunning views to izards alone and, in fact, although steep, the path poses no great difficulty.

Finding the beginning of this walk has caused readers plenty of problems over the years. The foolproof method now is to follow the Alternative walk and cross the Río Cinca by the bridge just south of the Parador de Monte Perdido, beside the Camping Municipal. This automatically puts you on the GR11 in the **Valle de Pineta**, which this walk follows. If you are staying in either of these places, this makes sense but means hiking 2km/1.2mi more than you have to *in each direction* (4km/ 2.5mi in total).

We prefer, when the river is not running high, to **start the walk** at the **Refugio de Pineta** (2km before the Parador). In this case you need to rockhop or wade across the river, depending on the amount of water, aiming a little to the south of a WATERFALL on the far side. Once across, pick up the well-trodden GR11 and follow it to the left.

Still wondering how to get up the sheer rock? In a few more minutes you will have the answer, as the cliff suddenly opens up to allow the path to enter the dense mixed forest, where it climbs steeply in a northwesterly direction.

Eventually you emerge into a CLEARING with a bewitching head-on view of the multi-tiered cliff faces of the **Tres Marías** waterfalls (**1h**). If it's in full flow, the stream below these waterfalls is safe to

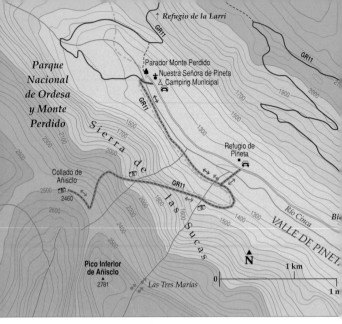

drink (you'll need all the water you can get). Cross the stream on rocks ... we once spotted a huge viper basking in the sun here. The path now dives back into predominantly beech forest and becomes even steeper, requiring you to use your hands in several places. After some **2h45min** the path emerges into a SECOND CLEARING, where there are some weirdly smooth cliffs above. (There's another opportunity to fill water bottles here.) Follow the path over the rocky shelves under the cliffs and up into an attractive meadow, where you might see izards. Beyond the pasture the path zigzags up the line of a slight ridge. The *parador* is now clearly visible below, and some strange isolated cliffs, looking like ruins, rise to your right. Sit for a while and enjoy the spectacle.

Then climb towards the pass, with ever more vertiginous views. If you have the energy to go all the way to the **Collado de Añisclo** (**4h30min**), you will be rewarded with glorious views of the Añisclo Canyon (Walk 25).

Descents sometimes take only half the time of ascents, but not in this case. Allow another *three hours* (**7h30min**) for the return, and don't be tempted to try any short cuts in the direction of the parador. The steep cliffs below you mean there are no short cuts!

In the Añisclo Canyon (Walk 25)

Walk 25: THE AÑISCLO CANYON

See photographs opposite and on page 29
Distance: 16km/10mi; 5h30min
Grade: easy climb of some 400m/ 1310ft, but sure-footedness and a head for heights essential
Equipment: no special equipment necessary — but see introductory notes on 'Walking', page 38.
How to get there and return:
🚗 The entrance to the canyon lies some 12.5km/8mi west of Escalona, along the road to Sarvisé (see Car tour 9). From June to mid-October, this road is one-way (east to west), so that if you are approaching from Sarvisé, you will have to make a 30 minute detour via Buerba and Puyarruego (compensated by wonderful views over the canyon).
Short walk: Walk as far as you like along the canyon and return by the same route; the first hour is easy and not vertiginous.
Useful contacts: Huesca Tourist Office 974 29 21 70 (www.huesca turismo.com); Parque Nacional de Ordesa y Monte Perdido 974 48 64 72, www.ordesa.com.

The massifs of Monte Perdido (the highest limestone mountain in Europe) and the Sierra de Guara to the south are riddled with canyons, of which the Ordesa (see Walk 26) is the largest and most famous. Some of the other gorges are accessible only to those who descend the falls using wet suits and ropes (giving rise to the sport of 'canyoning'). The Añisclo Canyon lies somewhere in between these extremes — it's intimate, but easy.

Start out from the parking place near the entrance to the **Añisclo Canyon**. Walk down the tarmac road (eastwards) until, after **4min**, you turn onto a track to the left, signposted *'PARQUE NACIONAL DE ORDESA Y MONTE PERDIDO'*. Cross the gorge by the concrete BRIDGE and continue on the track, which has a precipitous drop to the left. After **10min** pass a CAVE 'CHAPEL' to your right, above the confluence of the **Río Aso** and the **Río Vellos (Bellos)**. The track descends into the canyon to cross the Vellos by a concrete BRIDGE (**30min**). The route now narrows to a path that keeps the river on the right and begins to climb quite steeply.
After **40min** cross a side-stream on a metal BRIDGE. Another seven minutes brings you above an exciting-looking water chute — the sort 'canyoners' whoosh down (wearing protective clothing). After **1h** pass under an over-

hanging cliff. A further ten minutes brings you to a SPRING, where the water is safe to drink. The vegetation in the canyon is predominantly box, beech and oak — of which there are several types, including a Pyrenean variety which has white down on the undersides of the leaves.
After about **1h15min** reach a slightly 'delicate' part of the walk — a narrow, smooth and slippery section of rock with a steep fall to the right into the canyon below. On our first visit it was unguarded; on our last visit some none-too-solid looking posts and a wire had been erected. If you relax, there's no real difficulty. *Carefully* make your way to the far side. Climb past giant yew trees and reach a second (easier) gully crossing. The path gently undulates, keeping the precipitous drop to the right. The river flows below you — always within earshot. After **1h35min** you'll glimpse a

magnificent waterfall gushing through a narrow defile and, at the same time, another freshwater SPRING beside the path. A couple of minutes later come to a section of path which has been improved with logs and 'cobble'-stones. The path is very steep for the next 25 minutes, until it levels out in a small wood (**2h**).

Now you feel very high up, as you look down to the bottom of the gorge and the river far below. Grey and orange cliffs still tower above you, however. The path takes you round to the left,

Griffon vulture (above) and lammergier (left)

directly beneath these overhanging cliffs (here again the path has been secured with 'cobble'-stones). For the first time since entering the canyon, the path is not following the direct line of the river, but climbing in long zigzags up the wall of the gorge. At about **2h05min** come to a CONCRETE AND METAL BRIDGE (the remains of its much prettier wooden fore-runner can be seen below). Another steep climbing section zigzags for 35 minutes (**2h40min**), rising through conifers, fern and bracken, until the path emerges on a wide GRASSY PLATEAU with a steep unprotected drop to the right. After **2h55min** come to a rocky section over a stream (often dry), past giant beech trees and moss-covered rocks. This is followed by another 'roller-coaster' of ups and downs. The river comes into view again, and the way gradually descends towards the water's edge. Ahead are the spectacular mountains ringing the Ordesa Canyon. After **3h10min** you come to **La Ripareta**, the wide grassy plain shown on page 29, level with the river and surrounded by the canyon walls. Although we choose to end the walk here, it is possible to follow the path to the end of the canyon, reaching the waterfall known as Fon Blanca (add 2h *each way*).

To return, retrace steps to the SIGNPOST (**5h30min**).

Walk 26: ORDESA — THE GRAND CANYON WALK

See also photographs pages 2, 30-31, and cover

Distance: 16km/10mi; 5h30min

Grade: easy outward leg (ascent of 450m/1475ft). The return is more demanding (ascent of 250m/820ft and steep, stony descent of 700m/2300ft); those unnerved by heights should return by the outward route.

Equipment: stout shoes; but see also notes on 'Walking', page 38.

How to get there and return:
🚌 From Easter until mid-October there is a bus service from Torla to the Pradera de Ordesa (the starting point for the walk), beginning at 06.00 and finishing at 21.00, with a peak time frequency of 15 minutes, 974 48 64 66; or 🚙 (Car tour 9.) In summer (Easter to mid-October) motorists are obliged to park at Torla and take the bus service (see above). The rest of the year, motorists can use the Pradera de Ordesa car park which is the starting point for the walk. For any further information

Waterfalls near the Circo de Soaso

call the Parque Nacional de Ordesa y Monte Perdido at Torla (telephone 974 48 64 72, www.ordesa.com).

Short walk: Follow the footpath as far as the bridge (**Puente de Arripas**) above the **Cascada del Abanico**, then return along the opposite bank of the Arazas River (2h; easy, almost level walk).

Alternative walk: Extend the walk by climbing the **Circo de Soaso** to the **Refugio Góriz** (add 450m/1475ft; 2h30min return), where it is possible to stay the night (telephone 974 34 12 01, www.pyrenees-refuges.com). Surefootedness/head for heights essential. Notes page 114.

If you had to choose just one walk in the Pyrenees, this should be it, *but preferably outside the crowded peak summer weeks.* Amidst unforgettable canyon scenery, the track leads you to the foot of Monte Perdido, the third highest mountain in the range. The rocks themselves are a main attraction — endless calcareous cliffs, traversed by awesome stone balconies (known as *fajas*). But there is also the chance to see rare birds such as lammergeiers, griffon vultures and wallcreepers — while it is almost a certainty that you will spot izards (Pyrenean chamois).

Start out at the **Pradera de Ordesa** CAR PARK: take the track east (signposted 'CASCADAS COLA CABALLO'). It runs at a short distance from the **Río Arazas**, and the sheer canyon walls rise 1000 metres (almost 3500 feet) above you on both sides. At a crossing of paths, follow signs for 'SOASO/REFUGIO GORIZ'. After **10min** you'll glimpse on your left

the route to the Circo de Cotatuero — worth trying if you're in the area for several days, *but not if you suffer from vertigo!* The track, flat at first, continues under the dense canopy of a marvellous beech forest. The way then rises gently towards the **Cascada del Abanico** (**40min**), beyond which those doing the Short walk may cross the river.

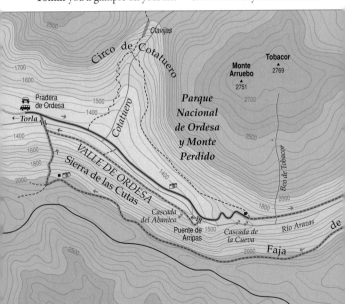

Río Arazas

From here the track climbs more steeply, eventually emerging from the dense part of the forest to spectacular views of the canyon walls above and a series of waterfalls below.

After **1h30min** the walk levels out, and you keep the attractive Río Arazas on your right. Soon the valley widens, and the huge bulk of Monte Perdido is ahead. After **2h15min** come to a REFUGE, from which the *circo* is now clearly visible — some 15 minutes' walking away. As you approach the **Circo de Soaso** (a rock amphitheatre associated with glaciation), the famous **Cascada de Cola de Caballo** comes into view to the left, looking — just as its name implies — exactly like a horse's tail (**2h30min**).

The main walk now returns along the **Faja de Pelay**, one of the famous rock shelves for which the canyon is renowned. After crossing the **Puente de Soaso*** the clearly marked path climbs slowly from the *circo* on the opposite side of the valley to your outward route. After 10 minutes (**2h40min**) there is a sign advising you not to start out after 15.00h

---

*If you are doing the Alternative walk, from the Puente de Soaso pick up the notes on page 114.

— you don't want to be negotiating this narrow path after dark. After 18 minutes (**2h48min**) the path levels out.

You pass above a tiered waterfall, the **Gradas de Soaso** (**3h**), with its clear green pools and foamy cascades, after which the path begins to climb more steeply. Watch out for loose stones. By **3h10min** you catch your first giddying glimpse of the car park, far, far below. The spectacular path continues through woods of birch, beech and pine until you arrive at a REFUGE AND VIEWPOINT (**4h36min**). You are now directly above the car park. The obvious descent past cliffs and through woods starts here. Be warned: the way is steep and stony, in several places badly eroded. You arrive back at the **Pradera de Ordesa** in **5h30min**.

Alternative walk — ascent to the Refugio Góriz

From the **Puente de Soaso** there are two ways up and onwards to the Refugio Góriz. You can choose between the scree path that zigzags up the side of the *circo* in a southeasterly direction, and the direct assault — via the *'clavijas'*. The former looks impossible, but is merely arduous; the latter looks miraculous, but is merely terrifying!

If you choose the scree, you will find that although the path is invisible from a distance, it is clear close-up, and marked at intervals with red and white paint stripes. The route via the *clavijas* involves a section assisted by a chain fixed to the rock by pegs and wire, and with a little of what climbers call 'exposure'. In reality, it isn't difficult, but anyone nervous of heights or carrying a heavy pack should stick to the scree path.

The two routes join up towards the top of the *circo* and, by either way, you will find yourself in **1h** on a broad shelf, with the radio mast of the Refugio Góriz just visible almost due north. This is an excellent spot for seeing izards, too, since they are accustomed to walkers here and don't flee as quickly as those in the more remote areas of the range … but don't waste their energy by trying to get too close to them.

Continue ascending the terraces in the general direction of the aerial, watching for red and white paint stripes (and sometimes flags, when there is snow on the ground).

The *refugio* gradually reveals itself nestling at the foot of Monte Perdido, at a height of 2160m/ 7085ft. In **1h30min** you can be enjoying a drink or a meal — or perhaps a bunk in one of the dormitories. The **Refugio de Góriz** is open all year; in winter the two guardians ski in with the provisions via the Cuello Gordo and the track to Nerin. In summer the hut can be bursting at the seams.

Walk 27: PIC D'ANIE

See also photograph page 32
Distance: 14km/8.7mi; 6h30min
Grade: moderate, but with a strenuous 1060m/3477ft of ascent for the full itinerary
Equipment: You will be climbing to 2504m/8213ft, so proper mountain walking equipment is essential (see introductory notes on 'Walking', page 38).
How to get there and return: The starting point is easily reached only by 🚗 (Car tour 10: at Lescun follow signs to the *gîte d'étape* and continue on a narrow but good track to a small parking area just before the refuge de Labérouat); otherwise 🚌 to Lescun-Cette-Eygun (service Pau — Canfranc: 08 36 35 35 35/freephone within France 08 05 90 36 35, www.sncf.com), then taxi (05 59 34 70 06) about 12km to the Refuge de

Labérouat (05 59 34 71 67).
Shorter walks: Turn back at the **Cabane du Cap de la Baigt** (2h return) or the **Col des Anies** (4h40min return).
Alternative walk: From the Cabane du Cap de la Baigt instead of taking the left-hand path, you can turn *right* and follow the GR10 north to the **Pas d'Azuns** (45min), followed by a slightly more testing 30 minute climb and scramble for the reward of spectacular views from the **Pas d'Osque** (1h15min from the *cabane*).
Other useful contacts: Vallée d'Aspe Tourist Office 05 59 34 57 57, www.aspecanfranc.com or www.tourisme-aspe.com; Lescun Maison de la Montagne 05 59 34 79 14 or 05 59 34 57 57, www.aspecanfranc.com or www.tourisme-aspe.com

There is a magic about Lescun and its setting — at the end of a winding road, looking out over fields to coniferous forests and, to the west, the startling limestone scenery of the Pic d'Anie region. (Car tour 10 takes you around the other

Looking east from the Col des Anies

side of the Pic d'Anie, where the limestone formations are even more incredible.) But perhaps the most magical thing of all is that brown bear are known to live somewhere here.

Start out from the **Refuge de Labérouat**. Pass in front of the refuge and after **2min** pick up the clear red and white paint flashes of the GR10, ignoring all other paths. The woods afford occasional glimpses of high mountains ahead and the bizarre cliffs of **Les Orgues de Camplong** to the right. In **55min**, just beyond the woods, you pass the **Cabane d'Ardinet**. By looking back down the valley you have just climbed you'll see the celebrated Pic du Midi d'Ossau in the far distance. Continue following the well-marked path until you arrive at the **Cabane du Cap de la Baigt** (1689m/5540ft; **1h15min**), where we leave the GR10. You can retrace your steps from here to return to your car in a total of 2h (Shorter walk).

Continue on the main itinerary by turning left (southwest) to follow the left bank of the stream (that is, keeping it on your left). After seven minutes (**1h22min**) cross the stream and continue zig-zagging up for just under 40 minutes, to arrive at a flat pasture with a SMALL LAKE (**2h**). The Pic d'Anie looms to the left. Continue along the path for another two minutes, at which point you will pass a large BROKEN LIMESTONE BLOCK. From here the path climbs steeply to the right, to join the scree slopes below the **Pic du Soum Couy**. Watch out for small cairn path markers and red and white flashes — you are now on the HRP. After just over half an hour you will arrive at the **Col des Anies** (2084m/6836ft; **2h 35min**), with an impressive view of Pic d'Arlas to the west. From here it's just 1.5km/0.9mi to the summit — but another 420m of

ascent! Leave the HRP and head southwards towards the summit of Pic d'Anie. The path has red waymarkings and occasional cairns. It curls around the west

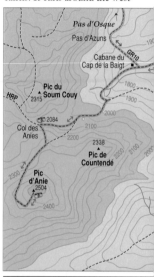

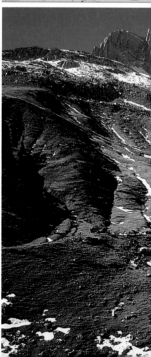

Right: Les Orgues de Camplong, near the Refuge de Labérouat; below: Pic de Coutendé

side of the peak, to attack the summit from the south.
From the **Pic d'Anie** (2504m/ 8213ft; **4h**) you will enjoy an immense panorama — as far as the sea on a clear day and to Vigne-

male in the opposite direction.
Return to **Refuge de Labérouat** by the same route (**6h30min**).

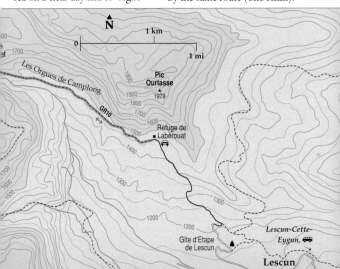

Walk 28: THE SONG OF ROLAND (MT ASTOBIZKAR)

Map continues overleaf
Distance: 16km/10mi; 5h35min
Grade: easy walking, with overall ascents of 420m/1380ft — but there are some sections where the path is indistinct and where good map reading skills would be helpful. See 'Equipment' below.
Equipment: A compass is recommended for those sections over limestone rubble, known locally as *lapiaz*, where the path is invisible. If you stray from the route in this generally open, rolling terrain, you can usually cut across the open countryside to get back on course.
How to get there and return: 🚗 From St-Jean-Pied-de-Port take the D301 to Estérencuby and, 3km/1.8mi further on, fork right onto the D428. After a further 7km/4.3mi, watch out for a track on the left which heads south to the nearby Col d'Orgambidé. Park on the grass just across the frontier (on the Spanish side of the col).
Short walk: From the **Col d'Arnostéguy** return directly to your car, following the main walk from the 4h15min-point (3h).
Useful contacts: St-Jean-Pied-de-Port Tourist Office 05 59 37 03 57, www.saintjeanpieddeport-paysbasque-tourisme.com; Taxis 05 59 37 13 37, 05 59 37 05 00 or 05 59 37 36 28 www.express.burricot.com

This is a walking geography and history lesson. The geography includes bizarre limestone scenery, while the history embraces cromlechs and a route that has variously been followed by the Romans during the conquest of northern Spain, pilgrims to Santiago, and Napoleon's troops. But, most famously of all, Charlemagne's army was ambushed here after the sacking of Pamplona, an event celebrated in the medieval poem, the *Song of Roland*.

Start out 200m to the south of the **Col d'Orgambidé:** follow a clear (but unwaymarked) track westwards. This quickly narrows

to a footpath and alternates between forest and open grassland where *dolines* (funnel-shaped depressions) and limestone rubble set traps for the unwary. The path becomes fainter and fainter as it climbs steadily along a small valley on the southern side of the frontier. Eventually the frontier is crossed between marker stones 207 and 208).

After **1h** a particularly large *doline* confirms that you are on course, forcing you leftwards, up a small hill. From the top you should be able to see the **Cabane d'Urculu**, a small house. Turn away from the *cabane* and head due south, climbing to a ridge and then on up to the SUMMIT of **Urculu** (1419m/

Memorial to Roland at the Puerto de Ibañeta

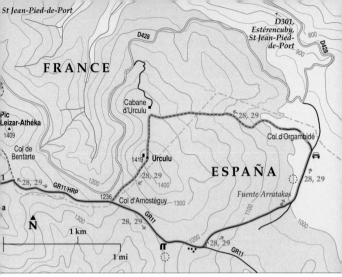

4654ft; **1h30min**). If you are in the right place you will be beside the low ruins of a stone tower, which some experts date from Roman times and others as late as 1500AD.

Descend southwest along the line of the frontier into the **Col d'Arnostéguy** (**1h40min**), where the D428 comes up from St-Jean-Pied-de-Port. *(Those following the Short walk can return from here by picking up the notes from the 4h15min-point below.)*

To continue the main walk, follow the GR11/HRP (red and white stripes) westwards along the French side of the frontier. After 30 minutes the path crosses to the Spanish side (**2h10min**), close to the **Col de Bentarte**. This is one possible site for the ambush of Charlemagne's rearguard.

Continue southwest along the route of the old Roman road (see map overleaf), past the ruined chapel of **Elizaxare** (**2h25min**). Where the trail cuts between two hills, break away to the right, to reach the SUMMIT of **Astobizkar** (1506m/4940ft; **3h**). Looking southwest from the top you will see the Puerto de Ibañeta, the most likely scene of the battle, where, in the *Song*, the dying

Roland tried to break his sword Durandel (and in so doing created the Brèche de Roland!; Walk 22). Now retrace your steps as far as the **Col d'Arnostéguy** (**4h 15min**). Here we follow the GR11 red and white waymarkings (and also blue flashes) along a dirt track heading eastwards into another COL (**4h30min**). About fifty paces off to the right is a RUINED DOLMEN and, a little further on, a CROMLECH of 16 stones, dating from about 2000BC.

After a further 20 minutes the GR11 brings you to four CABINS (**4h50min**). Just beyond them, abandon the GR11: at a DRINKING TROUGH, take the track to the left (northwards) signposted to the 'COLLADO DE AZPEGI, 1020M'. Eventually you pass a SPRING with another sign, 'FUENTE ARRATAKAS, 970M' (**5h20min**). Some 200m off to the left lies a second CROMLECH, this time of 11 stones. Continue along the track and regain your car at the **Col d'Orgambidé** after **5h35min**.

Walk 29: RONCESVALLES

See photograph page 118
Distance: 17km/10.5mi;
5h50min
Grade: easy walking, with overall
ascents of 500m/1640ft, but there
are some sections where the path
is indistinct and good map reading
skills would be helpful.
Equipment: A compass is recommended for those sections over
limestone rubble; see comments
for Walk 28 on page 118.
How to get there and return:
🚌 to Roncesvalles (948 30 02
87, www.autocaresartieda.com —
look for the Jaurrieta-Pamplona
service), from where you can
follow the path taken by pilgrims
returning from Santiago de
Compostela, heading northeast up
to the Collada Lepoeder. It is
waymarked with scallop shells (the
official sign for the pilgrimage
route). Add 500m/1640ft; 3h
return to the times given for
motorists. Or 🚗 taxi (05 59 37 36
28, www.expressburricot.com, or
948 23 23 00, www.taxipamplona.
com) to the Collada Lepoeder,
following the directions for

motorists below. For information
about public transport and taxis
telephone the Pamplona Tourist
Office: 948 42 04 20, www.
turismo.navarra.es. Or 🚗 (Car
tour 11); after visiting Roncesvalles, continue northwards and
just before the frontier, at the
Puerto de Ibañeta, turn right
along the tarmac road which leads
to the radio mast on Monte
Ortzanzurieta. After 2.5km/1.6mi
park at the Collada Lepoeder
(where a track goes off to the left).
Shorter walks
1) Follow the main walk to the
Col d'Arnostéguy and the
CROMLECH 15 minutes past it.
Then retrace your steps, but
deviate to the stone tower on
Urculu (4h return).
2) From **Roncesvalles**, follow
notes for those who come by bus
to reach the **Collada Lepoeder**.
Walk to **Astobizkar**, then return
and follow the road west to the
Puerto de Ibañeta (where you
will see the memorial to Roland
shown on page 118). From here a
waymarked path descends to

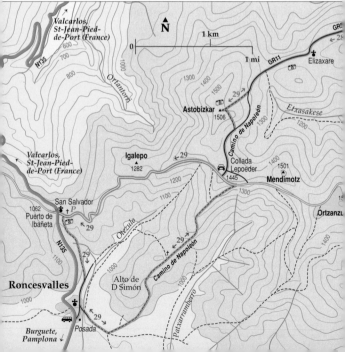

Roncesvalles (11km/6.8mi; 4h; easy, with an ascent of 550m/ 1800ft).
Useful contacts: Visitors Centre,

Burguete: 948 76 00 32, www.burguete.es; Monastery, Roncesvalles: 948 76 00 00, www.roncesvalles.es

Burguete was once the haunt of Ernest Hemingway, whose early novel, *Fiesta*, describes how he first saw 'the red roofs and white houses of Burguete … and away off on the shoulder of the first dark mountain … the grey metal-sheathed roof of the monastery of Roncesvalles'. Roncesvalles (Roncevaux to the French) claims relics of the battle, 'celebrated' in the medieval *Song of Roland*, that wiped out Charlemagne's rearguard. There is an excellent Visitors' Centre with an audio-visual history of Roncesvalles on the opposite side of the main road, facing the monastery.

Our timings start at the **Collada Lepoeder**: take the track heading northwards, known as the **Camino de Napoléon** (also the GR11).

where the D428 comes up from St-Jean-Pied-de-Port.
Now turn to the notes for Walk 28 and follow it from the

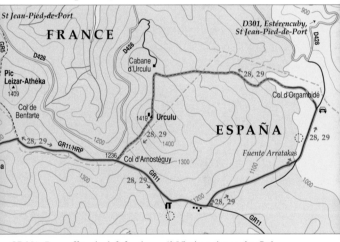

Bear off to the left for the SUMMIT of **Astobizkar** (1506m/ 4940ft; **10min**), where you join Walk 28. This is a brief resumé with the main timings for those starting from Collada Lepoeder. For a full description, refer to Walk 28.
From Astobizkar drop back down northeastwards over the grass to rejoin the track and, after following the red and white waymarks for 1h15min you will be at the **Col d'Arnostéguy (1h25min)**,

4h15min-point to the **Col d'Orgambidé (2h45min)**. Then pick up the instructions for the beginning of Walk 28, to bring you back to **Col d'Arnostéguy** once more (**4h25min**) and, from there, return to your car at the **Collada Lepoeder (5h50min)**.

Walk 30: IPARLA RIDGE

Distance: 10km/6.25mi; 6h30min

Grade: very strenuous if you go all the way to the top — 900m/2952ft of ascent

Equipment: the area is prone to mist; see 'Walking', page 38.

How to get there: 🚌 to Bidarray (Pont Noblia; SNCF Bayonne to St-Jean-Pied-de-Port line): 08 36 35 35 35/freephone within France 08 05 90 36 35, www.sncf.com), then cross the river by the bridge, turn left, and walk up to the *mairie* (town hall). or 🚗 (Car tour 12; park at the *mairie* in Bidarray (Pont Noblia). For a taxi telephone 05 59 37 40 81 or 05 59 37 78 71. For general information call the Hendaye Tourist Office 05 59 20 00 34, www.hendaye-tourisme.fr

To return:  from Bidarray (Pont Noblia), or 🚌
Short walk: Hike just far enough to enjoy the views and return the same way (about 3h return).
Alternative walk: Having reached the Pic d'Iparla, it is possible to continue along the ridge as far as the **Col d'Harrieta** (808m/ 2650ft), where you can quit the GR10 to take a waymarked path down to **Urdos**. Allow about 2h30min to descend from the Pic d'Iparla to Urdos (total 6h30min), from where you will have to take a taxi back to your car, or to a railway station (the nearest is St-Martin d'Arrossa, about 8km).

Iparla Ridge from near Bidarray

Bidarray

The Iparla Ridge (Crête d'Iparla) is a classic walk in the Basque country, the domain of black and griffon vultures. It is also part of the GR10 long-distance footpath, marked by red and white flashes.

Start out from the *mairie* at **Bidarray**. Walk up the hill, forking left (keeping the *gîte d'étape* to your right). After a few minutes the road divides again. Go right, climbing gently, until at **7min** you pass — and ignore — another turn to the right.

At **10min** follow a red footpath arrow round to the right, until you come to **Urdabordia**, a large farmhouse, where the tarmac ends (**15min**). Now join a wide earthen track which sweeps around to the left, through the farmyard and then becomes a steeply-climbing path marked with the red and white flashes of the GR10.

At **45min** you pass the first of what prove to be false trails to the right (merely the tracks made by animals and water). Continue on your path, occasionally over solid rock. Follow the red and white paint marks until you come to a RUIN (**55min**). The way is now clearly marked, climbing up the ridge with its all-round views, through woods, across a grassy bowl, and up to a HIGH POINT (**1h 45min**).

From now on you have the choice of sticking to the path along the cliff edge (**Crête d'Iparla**), for the frisson that comes with 'exposure', or of bearing away a little into the grass. Ignore the vultures wheeling overhead — it's nothing personal. If you've ever wondered what it's like to soar high above the ground on a *parapente*, the path to the summit will give you a fair idea. You can't go wrong — just follow the cliff. At the SUMMIT of **Pic d'Iparla** (1044m/3424ft; **4h**) your efforts are rewarded; the views are exhilarating — and terrifying.

Return the same way, or continue along the ridge for the Alternative walk. Whichever route you choose, you will be back down in either **Bidarray** or Urdos in about 2h30min (total **6h30min**).

Walk 31: CIRCUIT BASED ON BIRIATOU

Distance: 16km/10mi; 4h30min
Grade: moderate climb of 450m/1475ft
Equipment: water; see also introductory notes on 'Walking', page 38.
How to get there: 🚂 to Hendaye (Toulouse — Bayonne — Biarritz — St-Jean-de-Luz line): 08 36 35 35 35/freephone within France 08 05 90 36 35, www.sncf.com, then taxi: 05 59 37 40 81 or 05 59 37 78 71 to Biriatou. Or 🚗 (Car tour 12; park at Biriatou car parking area). For general information telephone the Hendaye Tourist Office 05 59 20 00 34, www.hendaye-tourisme.fr
To return: 🚗 taxi from Biriatou back to Hendaye station, or 🚗
Alternative walks: There are three itineraries described for this area. By referring to the map on pages 126-127 and Walks 32 and 33, you can make up your own alternatives.

Biriatou is a hill-top village notable for its splendid church (designated *'site classé'* in French conservation terms) and the unusual location of its *fronton* (pelota court) — it's joined onto the village *auberge*.

Start the walk at the CAR PARK in **Biriatou**, climbing the hill to the CHURCH and the *fronton* beside AUBERGE HIRIBARREN (both players and ball move like lightning so, if a game is in progress, watch out!). Take the alley beside the *auberge* and turn left onto a tarmac road. Notice — but ignore — a local walking sign to the right, marked 'Ibardin'. Its blue and white local footpath markings will become a regular feature during the day. After **8min**, at a sharp bend, take the path to the right, well-marked with both blue and white and red and white footpath flashes. This path divides almost immediately:

La Rhune from the Col d'Osin (Walks 31 and 32)

take the ascending path (again marked with both red and white and blue and white flashes — as well as a wooden sign detailing a local walk, 'THE LANCETTE'). After **12min** follow the path round to the right, where it narrows and swings in front of a concrete WATER-PUMPING STATION.

Ahead you'll see the cliffs of the **Rocher des Perdrix** ('Partridge Rock'), a wild landscape marred only by the giant electricity pylons. At **20min**, just under one of these pylons, the path divides. Take the clearly-marked, rather stony fork that leads uphill. After a few minutes this sweeps around to the

right, and the way now continues along the bottom of the cliffs. The path alternates between mud and stone, often with rocks and boulders 'cemented' into extra-ordinary pebble-dashed spheres, known as conglomerates.

After **40min** the footpath divides once more. Take the left-hand, ascending fork, marked in the red and white paint flashes of the GR10/Haute Route Pyrénées. At **1h** you arrive at a wide grassy plateau, the **Col d'Osin**. Walk over the pass in a fairly straight line. A clear view of a lake (sometimes dried up) opens up on your left.

At **1h10min** you arrive at the **Col des Poiriers** (photograph page 130). Those wanting a short walk can now turn left off the main path, head down to the lake, picnic and retrace their steps. Those continuing on the main walk should follow the path that keeps the small larch wood on the immediate right (ignore the track marked 'Lancette'). Here the marked path moves close to the wood and climbs for 15 minutes until it reaches a definite U-shaped dip, the **Col des Joncs** (**1h25min**). From here you enjoy new vistas southwards to the Bidasoa (Bidassoa in French) River.

At **1h40min** the red- and white-marked GR10/HRP swings sharply left, but you follow a new path to the right, almost immediately crossing a small stream. Follow this path until, at **1h50min**, you reach an impressive ridge with splendid views all around. Your walk takes you to the right here, but those with an interest in military history could take a ten-minute diversion to the left, to see the *ancien redoute* (fortified stronghold) de la Bayonnette. Close by is frontier stone 9, a place where you can straddle the Franco-Spanish border (see photograph page 131). Return to the ridge-top crossroads where you started your diversion and follow the line of the ridge southwest as it descends towards the valley and the **Bidasoa River**.

Continue descending and note a number of good vehicle tracks joining from the Spanish side. You do not want any of these, however tempting they may look; stay instead on the blue- and white-marked path, reaching an old RUIN

at **2h25min**. After about five minutes of gentle descent, come to a PLANTATION OF OAKS (**2h30min**). Here the path starts to descend much more steeply, in places becoming quite difficult. You'll notice footpath paint flashes on trees.

At the bottom of the path you may have to negotiate a FENCE — either by a stile or by climbing over. Then turn right along a vehicle track, almost immediately fording a stream. Continue to follow the track, with the stream on your right. The track is flat at first but then zigzags up to a farm called 'LIZARLAN' (**3h30min**). Continue from here to a tarmac road (**4h**) and follow it straight ahead. At about **4h20min** blue and white flashes on your right announce a narrow path that climbs up obliquely from the road, through trees, to regain the CHURCH and CAR PARK at **Biriatou** (**4h30min**).

Walks 31 and 32: fields near Biriatou

Walk 32: CHOLDOKOGAGNA (XOLDOKOGAIÑA)

See also photograph on page 125

Distance: 15km/9.5mi; 4h10min

Grade: easy climbs totalling about 600m/1970ft

Equipment: no special equipment necessary — but see introductory notes on 'Walking', page 38.

How to get there: 🚂 to Hendaye; then 🚗 taxi or car to

Biriatou (see Walk 31). However, it is possible to shorten the walk some 2.5km/1h by starting at the Col d'Ibardin: follow *Walk 33*, but turn right when you rejoin the track beyond the short-cut path (at about 27min).

To return: same transport from Biriatou or the Col d'Ibardin

Alternative walks: See Walk 31.

The highest peak in the Basque country, La Rhune, is unfortunately spoilt for walkers by its rack railway and radio mast. Try instead this delightful itinerary: it takes you through a varied landscape to a panoramic viewpoint.

FOLLOW WALK 31 as far as the **Col des Poiriers** (**1h10min**). At the pass, take the track off left down to the lake and follow it along the southern shore, through tree plantations. It climbs to join a well-made track coming from the right (**1h45min**). Turn left and follow this new track for eight minutes (**1h53min**), until a further track comes up, heading obliquely back left, towards the

dam. Follow this track to the DAM (**1h58min**), cross it, and then take a track heading right (north). It runs along the side of a valley, above the **Arolako Erreka River**. The way at first falls, but then climbs towards a RADIO MAST on the top of a ridge, reached some 30 minutes from the dam (**2h30min**).

Cross over the ridge, turning left in front of the mast, and drop

down onto the tarmac road on the other side. Follow the tarmac in a hairpin bend away from the mast, to a grassy PARKING AREA (**2h35min**).

From here several trails lead off, and the confusion is not helped by the apparent lack of signs or waymarks. The path you want leaves the parking area in a south-southwesterly direction. It climbs towards the summit of a mountain (Choldokogagna), but keeps the ridge a little to the left. You will pick up blue and white paint marks on the ground almost at once so, if you haven't seen any after three or four minutes, you'll know you are on the wrong path. Follow the paint waymarks until, 45 minutes from the parking area, you reach the rounded summit of **Choldokogagna** (also called Xoldokogaiña; 486m/1595ft; **3h20min**). After enjoying the views to the sea and inland to La Rhune and beyond, descend southeast on the clear path that leads back to the **Col d'Osin**

Walks 31, 32, 33: At the Col des Poiriers

(**3h30min**). Having regained your outgoing route, bear right to retrace your steps to **Biriatou** (**4h10min**).

Walk 33: COL D'IBARDIN

See map opposite; see also photograph opposite
Distance: 8km/5mi; 2h15min
Grade: easy climb of some 200m/650ft
Equipment: no special equipment necessary
How to get there and return: The Col d'Ibardin is a mini-Andorra on the Franco-Spanish frontier, a place the French love to visit for weekend shopping expedi-

tions. Reach it by taxi (943 63 33 03, www.radiotaxibidasoa.com, or 05 59 37 40 81 or 05 59 37 78 71) or in your own car (🚗) by taking the D4 and D404 from the coastal strip between Hendaye and St-Jean-de-Luz (via Urrugne and Herboure), by the road up from Spain via Vera de Bidasoa, or as a detour from Ascain (Car tour 12).
Alternative walk: See Alternative walk 31, page 125.

The Col d'Ibardin is on the famous Haute Route Pyrénées, but we suggest an easy itinerary that everyone can enjoy. It takes you through magnificent plantations and around a lake.

Start out just before the shops in the main shopping street (a cul-de-sac) at the **Col d'Ibardin**: take an excellent track leading off to the right. A CHAIN prevents vehicles entering (since it would otherwise be a marvellous way of avoiding French customs), but it is open to ramblers. You'll come upon a picnic place within five minutes, but it is a little over-used.
The level track winds among magnificent — if somewhat too regimented — plantations, and later beside a beautiful oak forest. In **25min** you have your first glimpse of a lake ahead and, a minute later, a blue and white arrow indicates a short-cut to the

left. You'll rejoin a track in another minute or two. Turn left on this track and follow it among the plantations, keeping the LAKE on your right. In **1h** you reach the **Col des Poiriers** beyond the lake, where you meet up with Walks 31 and 32.
To return to the Col d'Ibardin, turn left at the Col des Poiriers and skirt the larch forest, following Walk 31 (page 128) as far as the **Ancien Redoute de la Bayonnette** (**1h50min**). From the *redoute* continue northeast, more or less along the ridge, until you regain the shopping area at the **Col d'Ibardin** (**2h15min**).

Walkers near frontier stone 9 and the Ancien Redoute de la Bayonnette, looking south towards the Peñas de Haya in Spain (Walks 31 and 33)

Walk 34: PEÑAS DE HAYA (AIA)

Distance: 3km/2mi; 3h (12km/7.5mi; 5h if you descend to Irún).

Grade: unlike most other walks in this book, this itinerary involves some rock-climbing, albeit of a fairly easy kind. For the full itinerary, you'll need your hands, agility and a head for heights. The highest peak is about 330m/1082ft above the parking area but, allowing for all the ups and downs, you'll do about 480m/1575ft of ascent.

Equipment: suitable gripping footwear is essential; stout trainers are fine, but shoes with smooth soles must *not* be worn.

How to get there: train to Irún (RENFE 902 24 34 02, www.renfe.com); then taxi (943 63 33 03, www.radiotaxibidasoa.com) from Irún station. Ask the taxi driver for the Peñas de Haya (Aia), then watch out for the parking spot suggested below for motorists. Or 🚗 (Car tour 12): Motorists approaching Irún from the French border on the N1

should turn left at the first roundabout and, at the second roundabout (only a short distance from the first), go straight over. Pass Barrio Meaka and continue for a further 5km/3mi, ignoring side turnings, until the road, having climbed towards the summit of the Peñas de Haya, begins to descend again and passes under electricity cables. If you are in the right spot you will see that there is a parking area with a signboard.

To return: Return on foot to Irún station by one of the footpaths described below; car drivers regain their vehicles at the parking.

Short walk: Those without a taste for rock-climbing can follow the itinerary as long as they feel comfortable, returning the same way.

Alternative walk: Paths skirting the peaks to the east and west are detailed on the signboard.

Useful contacts: Irún Tourist Office 943 02 07 32, www.basquecountry-tourism.com; www.bidasoaturismo.com

The Peñas de Haya (Aia) are a landmark on the Spanish side of the border and a great spectacle, known to the French as the 'Trois Couronnes' — the three crowns. They are very popular with climbers, offering routes of various degrees of difficulty, as you will see on the signboard at the parking area. Our itinerary follows paths suitable for fit, agile walkers and does not require special equipment or skills, other than a head for heights. We are going to walk and scramble right along the spine of the three peaks, returning by a path just below the summits to the west. If you have a fear of heights, just do the first part, or follow one of the lower itineraries shown on the board.

Start out from the PARKING AREA WITH SIGNBOARD below the **Peñas de Haya**: follow the obvious path that heads southeastwards towards the peaks. After **12min** come to a PILLBOX and follow the well-trodden path that zigzags beyond it, to arrive on a minor summit, **Muganix** (786m/2580ft; **30min**). But you are not yet on one of the three peaks of Aia! For that privilege, drop down and continue along the ridge. The path passes an area where the rock is sharply

tilted and the soil below to the left eroded into CAVES, while to the right there is an impressive drop. At **40min** the path divides; take the upper way, across an easy slab of rock, and come to the next summit, where a shrine announces '**Monte Irumugarrieta**, 806 metres' (2645ft; **45min**). Congratulations! You have bagged your first Aia summit.

To continue along the ridge, drop back down over the rock slab to where the path divided and now take the lower path onward and up **Monte Txurrumurru** (826m/2710ft; **1h**).

From here on things get more tricky because there is a steep descent into a gully — and descents are always more unnerving that ascents. If it's not for you, turn back. Otherwise, climb down into the gully and up the opposite side, following the path along the ridge. At the far end the path zigzags down in a southeasterly direction to meet another path coming from the northeast, along a kind of 'toboggan run'. From here you climb southwestwards in a series of zigzags to the final summit, **Erroilbide** (836m/2745ft — also known as Monteaya; **1h30min**). The views

Peñas de Haya (Aia)

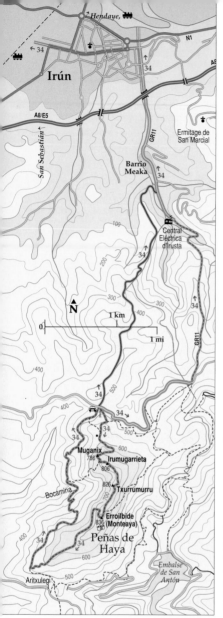

due south above the trees and along a shelf, before once more descending to join the path coming from the Aritxulegi tunnel. Turn right (northwards) along this path, which cuts through the trees and across the bottom of the gully known as the **Corredor de Bocamina**, to return to the PARKING AREA in 1h30min (**3h**).

Walking on down to Irún

If you came by taxi, there are two possible routes to take you back to Irún. You can take a track that begins on the opposite side of the road from the parking area, by the electricity pylon. The track is loosely surfaced and in places descends steeply.

But the easiest route to follow is the GR11 footpath, which is marked by red and white stripes. To pick that up, walk along the road eastwards from the parking area for about 1.3km/0.8mi (**3h 20min**) Go *past* the GR11 footpath where it joins the road from the right, continue for two minutes, and then follow the GR11 where it descends to the left. In about 40 minutes (**4h**) you will find yourself at the **Central Eléctrica d'Irusta**, just beyond which you can join the road for **Irún** and the STATION (**5h**).

over the sweep of Basque coastline from San Sebastián to Biarritz are superb.

You could return by retracing your steps, but we suggest taking the path that descends in zigzags to the northeast until, at a height of around 700m, it swings almost

● Index

Geographical names only are included here; for non-geographical entries, see Contents, page 3. A page number in *italic type* indicates a map reference; a page number in **bold type** a photograph or drawing; both may be in addition to a text reference on the same page. To save space, the following are indexed separately: mountains; cols; caves; rivers, valleys, gorges.

135